MIDLAND LOCOMOTIVES

Old No. 1273 is seen here as LMS No. 1247 when photographed on 19th November 1931. When this picture was taken the locomotive was employed on trials between Buxton and Millers Dale with the Hudd ATC system, later to be installed on the LT & S Section. A further view of this engine is at *Plate 27*.

National Railway Museum

AN ILLUSTRATED REVIEW OF

MIDLAND LOCOMOTIVES

FROM 1883

BY

R. J. ESSERY & D. JENKINSON

VOLUME THREE

TANK ENGINES

WILD SWAN PUBLICATIONS LTD.

ISBN 0 906867 66 5

SUPPLEMENTARY INFORMATION TO VOLUME TWO

Plate	
1	77A, Bradford F. Square 18.3.05.
29	902, Leeds 1905.
30	132A, Kentish Town shed.
42	139, Buxton.
57	1505, Holbeck shed.
58	1301, Cheltenham.
64	280, Derby – acting station pilot, north end.
65	211, Carnforth Midland, stored (note Western Division '36' plate).
69	Belle Vue shed (185).
71	204 (4 = Worcester plate), Up at Kings Norton, 8.1919.
72	205, Nottingham Midland.
75	254, Walsall.
77	250, Derby station, north end pilot (ex Works).
79	209, inside Carnford Mid shed (note Western Division '36' plate).
89	1338, Leeds Wellington.
127	372, Derby shed, ex Works.
150	'H' 4–4–0, Kentish Town shed.
174	485, Manchester Central.
178	527, Kentish Town shed.
187	181, Cheltenham Spa Lansdown.
188	123, St. Pancras.
190	1856, St. Pancras.
195	1859, Kentish Town shed, 4.1904.
201	600, Derby shed.
202	600, coming into Derby from Chaddesden sidings.
207	Lincoln St. Marks 20.2.1923. (Headlamp reads 'MR 640, Nottingham').
227	690, Kentish Town shed.
228	691, Kentish Town shed.
229	685, Kentish Town shed.
239	759, St. Pancras.
241	735, Derby – opposite station (Works offices in rear); date 7.9.1912. Note 8-wheeled tender.
242	719, Kentish Town shed.
249	2788, Kentish Town shed.
253	769, Kentish Town shed, 23.7.1921.
254	720, Nottingham Midland.
255	726, Millhouses shed.
256	733, Kentish Town shed.
258	40741, Bristol shed, 17.8.1951.
260	705, Trafford Park shed.
261	706, Trafford Park shed.
263	700, Birmingham New Street, 9.10.1913.
266	717, Kentish Town shed.
267	726, Trafford Park shed.
270	744, Derby station, north end.
271	740, Holbeck shed.
277	768, Manchester Central.
280	777, Manchester Central.
290	993, Leicester London Road, 1.1.1910.
292	1003, Nottingham Midland – date confirmed as 1908 (taken by F. H. Gillford).
293	1005, St. Pancras.
295	1044, Kentish Town shed, 19.5.1923.
298	1040, Kentish Town shed.
302	1038, Kentish Town shed.
307	M1000, Derby shed, 22.5.1948.
309	1000, Derby shed.
312	2634 (with tender 821), Holbeck shed.
316	1013, Kentish Town shed.
318	1006, Leeds Wellington station.
322	1010, Derby shed.
324	1027, Kentish Town shed.
328	995, Holbeck shed.
330	999, Durran Hill shed, 11.4.1927.
331	808, Derby shed.

ERRATA TO VOLUME TWO

As far as we can see very few errors remain undetected in Volume 2. Those which have come to light are given below.

Page	
viii	For 1944 read 1924.
x	No. 1402 is at Carnforth not Lancaster.
45	We failed to credit A. G. Ellis.
85	The '1562' class rebuilding did not begin until 1906, not 1904 as stated.
135	Table 11. The correct date for Orders 2676A and 2676B was 1906 not 1904.
193	Under Tender Rebuilding *Plate 243* should read *Plates 262/3.*

Designed by Paul Karau
Typesetting by Berkshire Publishing Services
Printed and bound by Butler & Tanner Ltd., Frome

Published by
WILD SWAN PUBLICATIONS LTD.,
1-3 Hagbourne Road, Didcot, Oxon, OX11 8DP

CONTENTS

This view of old No. 2620, which was to become MR/LMS No. 1420, illustrates an example of the final series of 0–4–4Ts built in 1900. *National Railway Museum*

The ubiquitous Midland Railway open cab shunting engine is represented here by engine No. 2001 (later to become No. 1833 in 1907) when it was photographed in lined crimson lake livery c.1900. *Authors' Collection*

INTRODUCTION

In this volume, we continue our detailed analysis of the Midland Locomotive fleet by considering all of those tank engine designs which eventually reached the LMS. Once again, these are predominantly from the Johnson and later periods plus a few of the older types which enjoyed a long life. For reasons previously stated, our coverage is generally confined to the Midland's red engine period and we shall continue to concentrate on the many and various changes to their external appearance.

For reasons which we explained in the introduction to Volume 2, this particular offering is one of the 'extra' volumes which the publisher has kindly agreed to insert into the series. Because it was already written as part of the originally envisaged Volumes 2 and 3, we are able to offer it in the same year as our survey of passenger tender types and we fully expect that for much the same reasons, the publisher will also be able to allow the freight tender engines to follow within a further twelve months.

The Midland Railway was not a great tank engine line, so this volume is inevitably rather slimmer than the last, but this has allowed us, by way of bonus, to find space also to offer some further comments about Midland locomotive design and building policy at the end of the class chapters. In terms of subject matter, these observations could well have been included in Volume 1, save that they have only recently come to light as a result of recent research into the NRM archives, partly by one of the authors, but particularly by the museum librarian, Philip Atkins. We are very pleased indeed that Phil should have agreed to let us incorporate his research into this book and are happy to acknowledge his scholarship. We are even happier that his findings tend to reinforce some of our more speculative comments in Volume 2!

Apart from Phil Atkins and, of course, John Edgington and the rest of the library staff at the NRM, we must also, yet again, express our especial gratitude to two other stalwarts without whose help this series could well have been stillborn: Bernard Mathews for the continued total access to his splendid photographic collection which we have 'picked over' time and time again; and Stephen Summerson whose advice and comment has proved to be invaluable, to say nothing of his patience in reading through the manuscripts of all these volumes and amplifying many points on the way with unfailing courtesy. We also owe considerable thanks to many others who have helped us in one way or another, be it with pictures, by providing us with drawings (often newly made), or simply offering us advice and guidance. These include: Roy Anderson, Roger Carpenter, H. C. Casserley, Gordon Coltas, A. G. Ellis, Vic Forster, Geoff Goodfellow, L. Hanson, the Historical Model Railway Society, Bill Stubbs, David Tee, Peter Truman, A. E. West and Ken Woodhead. In addition we express our thanks to Steven Essery who has continued to turn the many changed manuscripts into typescript for the printer.

We hope readers will continue to enjoy our story but we must stress that ours is the sole responsibility for errors and omissions and again we invite comments and/or corrections (via the publisher) so that a final corrective appendix can be included in the last volume.

RJE
Solihull
1988

DJ
Knaresborough
1988

NOTES ON THE USE OF THIS BOOK

OTHER PUBLISHED REFERENCES

To save space and cost, we have not thought it necessary to fill the pages with great lists of numbers and neither have we included over-long technical specifications. In these two areas we have given the minimum information consistent with positive identification of type. However, we do think that readers who wish for more in this area will find the following books quite useful: *Derby Works and Midland Locomotives*, J. B. Radford, Ian Allan 1971; *British Locomotive Catalogue 1825-1923 Vol. 3A* by D. Baxter, Moorland Publishing 1982 (Note: this volume does contain errors so treat with caution); *Midland Railway Locomotive Album*, Robin Higgins, Vintage Carriage Trust; *S. W. Johnson, Midland Railway Locomotive Engineer Artist*, Jack Braithwaite, Wyvern Publishing; *Locomotive and Train Working in the Nineteenth Century*, E. L. Ahrons, reprinted from various issues of *The Railway Magazine*; *The Midland Railway*, Hamilton Ellis, Ian Allan.

DIAGRAMS/DRAWINGS

We have included a number of diagrams and drawings in the text. Some of the drawings have been specially prepared and may be considered accurate, others have been used before. The diagrams are less helpful in this respect, often being deficient in detail and at times incorrect, sometimes embracing more than one visible variant within a wheel arrangement. However, they do assist in providing a convenient 'shorthand' identification (below). Indeed a skilled draughtsman armed with a General Arrangement drawing before rebuilding may, with the aid of the diagram, photographic and other information, be able to produce a drawing for a class which was never the subject of an 'official general arrangement detailed drawing'!

IDENTIFICATION OF TYPE (ALL VOLUMES)

This subject is more thoroughly covered in Chapter 1 of Volume 2 but our normal method of identification of class, other than by wheel arrangement, is to quote the first running number allocated, e.g. '1400' class for the celebrated 6 ft. 9 in. Johnson 2–4–0s. This method is used throughout, where relevant, supplemented by references to engine diagram number(s) and/or subsequent 'popular' designations, if thought helpful in context, e.g. 'Compound', 'Belpaire', etc.

LOCOMOTIVE NUMBERING

Where engines were involved in the great 1907 renumbering (by wheel arrangement and power class see Volume 1, page 22) both numbers are quoted where necessary. In general, the *final* pre-1907 number is regarded as definitive in the case of engines which had carried several numbers prior to the big 1907 re-organisation. A full 1907 renumbering list is in Volume 1, page 187. In point of fact, virtually all the engines covered in this book carried 1907 numbers, and for some of them, of course, this was the only number anyway.

POWER CLASS

Although numerical assessment of power was not adopted in its final form until the 20th century, it is difficult to write about MR engines at any period without reference to their subsequent power designation(s). This has been done wherever it seems helpful to understanding. Power class references can always be distinguished from numerical class designations by the fact that the power class figure (1 to 4) always *follows* the word 'class'. Thus, for example, while '483' class is a designation of a specific type, class 2 is a definition of power, which could and did embrace several types.

LIVERY

The description of liveries is covered in detail in Volume 1, including a list of abbreviated definitions of the styles on page 114. This method of livery summary will be adopted throughout this volume and, for convenience, the definitions relevant to this part of the work are repeated below:

MR Green – Pre-November 1883 livery. Could be either Kirtley Dark or Johnson Light Green.

Early Crimson Lake – Implies the pre c.1890 period when certain 'below the footplate' lining was not present.

Full and 'Decorated' Crimson Lake – Implies the period c.1890-1905 when additional lining was used below the footplate and elsewhere. While extra lining was universally used, the term 'decorated' is particularly appropriate when describing the ornate additional lining used by certain paintshops during the mid/late 1890s until after the turn of the century. This additional lining was most frequently applied to the more important passenger locomotives but was also placed on certain tank engines.

Simplified Crimson Lake or Deeley livery – Describes the simplified lining practices introduced by Deeley c.1905 which saw the level of lining gradually reduced over a 2-3 year period to less than that used during the Early Crimson Lake livery period. During this period black was introduced to replace the red used hitherto for wheels and the outside of the frames. This term also covers the LMS 1923-28.

Locomotive Brown/Plain Crimson Lake/Brick Red – These descriptions apply to the various 'Utility Red' styles used for certain goods engines (see page 97 Volume 1.

Plain Black – MR/LMS/BR black without lining.

Intermediate Passenger Livery – This describes the black livery with red lining introduced in 1928 by the LMS for many locomotives which hitherto had been painted Crimson Lake.

Full BR Livery – Describes the lined black LNWR style livery adopted by British Railways and applied to certain ex-MR passenger locomotives (tender and tank).

WHEEL DIAMETERS (ALL VOLUMES)

For a given wheel arrangement, the driving wheel diameter is often a useful differentiation of type (e.g. the 0–4–4T. Although driving wheel diameters are normally quoted to the nearest half-inch, there is, in fact, no significant difference (beyond tyre thickness) between, for example, nominal 7 ft. 0 in. and 7 ft. 0½ in. wheels, both of which sizes could have been worn down to about 6 ft. 10 in. or less after a typical lifespan before new tyres were fitted. Indeed, because of the effect of tyre wear, there is a strong case for disregarding wheel diameter differences which were less than 3 inches and there is certainly no cause fo the pedant to get too neurotic about this matter. However, since changes in nominal driving wheel diameter frequently caused changes in *visual* characteristics (e.g. splasher dimensions on the 0–4–4T), there is a case for considering them with reasonable accuracy. This we have tried to do.

It should be noted that some other records give differing wheel dimensions (usually varying by ½ in.). For reasons explained in Chapter 1, Volume 2, most of our dimensions (where applicable) are taken from the company's 1903 reference.

LOCOMOTIVE DETAILS

Small variations in detail as they affected MR engines 'across the board' are covered in Volume 1, Chapter 3, and their substance will not be repeated in this volume. However, where relevant, changes from the 'norm' will be discussed in the class chapters.

SEQUENCE OF TREATMENT

Most chapters give a general review followed by a more detailed class-by-class survey. In the analysis of each class, a consistent order of treatment will, in general, be followed, namely:

1. Date and number built, including original running numbers and a summary of the class as handed over to the LMS in 1923.
2. Analysis of visual characteristics 'as built' (or, in the case of pre-1883 designs, 'as at 1883').
3. Subsequent visual changes as a result of rebuilding (if any) after 1883.
4. Liveries carried during MR period (with examples).

Old No. 799, a Dübs-built engine, is seen here at Victoria in May 1909 carrying the appropriate headcode for working into this station. *National Railway Museum*

PRE-1903 LAMP IRON POSITIONS

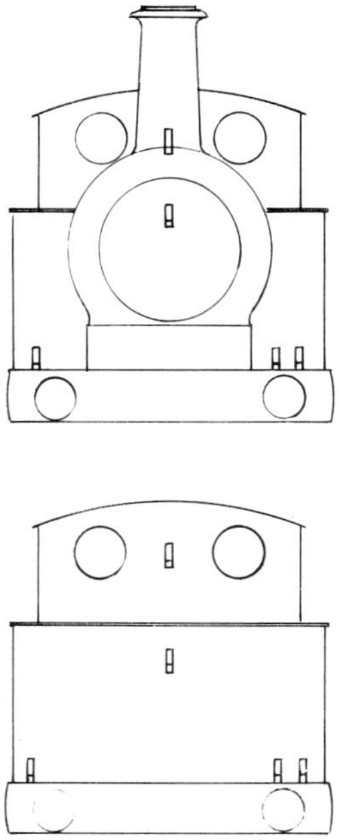

'1102' class locomotive No. 1106A (later No. 1624) at Devynock on the Neath and Brecon Railway with a Midland Railway goods train c.1900. *Authors' Collection*

This drawing and photograph illustrate the pre-1903 lamp iron positions on a closed cab engine. On an open cab tank engine, as far as we know, only the four bunker rear lamp iron positions were used. However, on the Johnson cab there was a socket for the driver's hand lamp. This was located centrally at the rear of the cab roof and so could, if need be, carry the driver's lamp in order to show the two vertical lamp positions. The pre-1903 lamp iron arrangement for tenders was shown at Fig. 19, page 92, Volume 2.

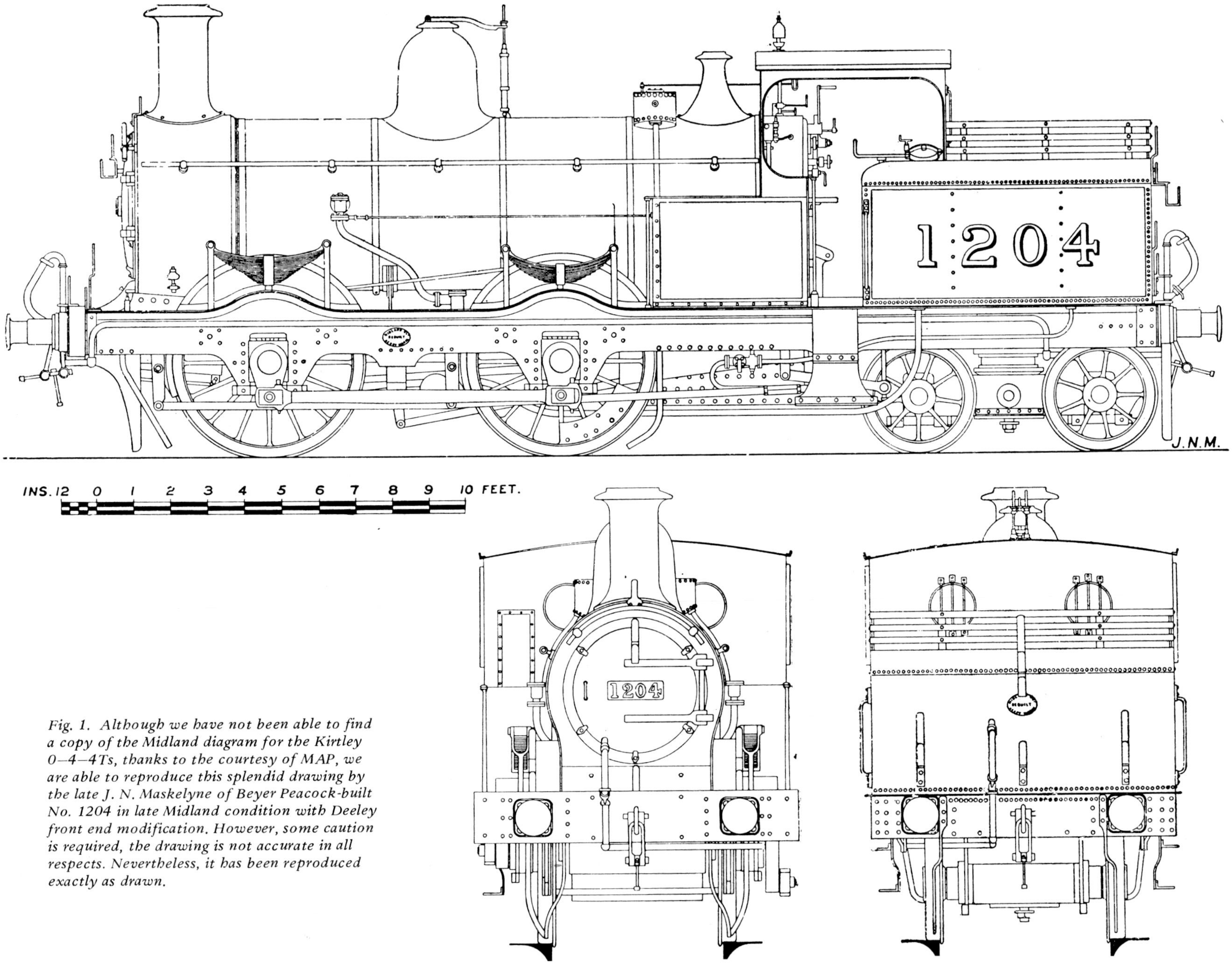

Fig. 1. Although we have not been able to find a copy of the Midland diagram for the Kirtley 0–4–4Ts, thanks to the courtesy of MAP, we are able to reproduce this splendid drawing by the late J. N. Maskelyne of Beyer Peacock-built No. 1204 in late Midland condition with Deeley front end modification. However, some caution is required, the drawing is not accurate in all respects. Nevertheless, it has been reproduced exactly as drawn.

CHAPTER ONE

KIRTLEY AND JOHNSON 0-4-4T CLASSES

BY contrast with its passenger tender engine fleet, wherein were contained three wheel arrangements (four, if one adds the 2—2—2s), not to mention numerous varieties of style within each wheel arrangement, the Midland's passenger tanks seem in retrospect to have been of sublime simplicity! Until Deeley's time, only one truly standard wheel arrangement, the 0—4—4T, was favoured and Deeley only contributed one further type — the 0—6—4T (see Chapter 2). Even the few 'Metropolitan' 4—4—0Ts (described in Volume 6) scarcely changed the picture.

All told, therefore, the 0—4—4T was the typical Midland passenger tank and eventually came to number some 231 examples, all but 26 of which were to the Johnson pattern. There was, in consequence, a basic degree of homogeneity in the passenger tank field quite different from the fascinating variety to be seen amongst the tender engines (Vol. 2). There were, of course, many subtle variations to be seen, but essentially the MR passenger tanks were quite a tidy lot.

The concept began, as did many things Midland, during the reign of Mathew Kirtley and it is with his legacy that we start this review.

THE KIRTLEY 0-4-4Ts 690 AND 780 CLASSES

Summary

690 CLASS

Built by Beyer Peacock 1869.
Original Midland Railway numbers 690-695.
Transferred to the duplicate list in 1898 as 690A-695A.
Midland Railway 1907 numbers 1200-1205, all to LMS.
In 1930 No. 1201 was renumbered 1212 and No. 1203 became No. 1213.
Class extinct 1934.

780 CLASS

Built by Dübs & Co. 1870.
Original Midland Railway numbers 780-799.
Nos. 780-783 to the duplicate list as 780A-783A in 1898.
Midland Railway 1907 numbers 1206-1225, all except No. 1212 to LMS.
Class extinct 1935.

The Kirtley 0—4—4T was that somewhat unusual creature, a 'back' tank. In this type of engine, the water was carried in a bunker tank at the rear of the locomotive.

They were built in 1869-70 by two outside contractors (6 by Messrs. Beyer-Peacock and 20 by Dübs & Co.) and initially displayed a weatherboard like the majority of Kirtley engines. It was in this guise that they existed at the start of our period of survey (*Plate 1*). During the late 1890s, Johnson began fitting 'all-over' cabs and this alteration turned out to be the most noticeable change of appearance which they ever underwent, replacement Johnson boilers notwithstanding.

The two series of engines were given different class designations and throughout their lives, the two batches could readily be distinguished. The Beyer-Peacock engines had straight-sided bunkers and were devoid of a running plate (footplate) angle iron; whereas the Dübs engines had flared tops to the bunker side and a small, but quite noticeable footplate angle iron. In addition, there were other minor differences. All 26 were originally condenser fitted and, until this feature was subsequently removed from some of them, a third difference in appearance between the two series could be seen in the shape and configuration of the condenser pipes. These differences are well shown in *Plates 2 & 3*.

The fitting of the all-over Johnson cabs usually went, as was typical at this time, with the replacement of the original boiler with a Johnson Class 'C', as fitted to many Johnson 0—4—4Ts, and the sporting of the characteristic Johnson chimney. Thus they remained, more or less, until Deeley began the customary 'front end' changes c.1907; but even when this had happened (e.g. *Plate 4*), the general characteristics of these double-framed engines remained much as they had always been.

In one respect, the Deeley front end modification was at first a little unusual in that the separate smokebox handrail (always a feature of these engines) remained of curved style (*Plate 5*) and it was not until considerably later — generally in LMS days — that the more customary straight handrail appeared (*Plate 6*).

Condensing apparatus, originally fitted from new for working trains over the underground lines between Moorgate and Kentish Town, began to be removed from many engines during Fowler's time, but quite a few retained the apparatus until LMS days (*Plate 6*). Two engines (MR Nos. 1201/3) were renumbered 1212/3 in 1930 by the LMS to make way for absorbed ex- S & DJR 0—4—4Ts.

Plate 1. Dübs-built 0–4–4T No. 785 (later No. 1211) is seen in green livery with rudimentary weatherboard - cum - cab roof and Johnson chimney at about the start of the 1880s. Built in 1870, the engine was rebuilt in 1892 and lasted until 1935. This is a fairly typical condition for the Kirtley 0–4–4Ts at the start of our more detailed survey.
Authors' Collection

The Midland liveries applied to the Kirtley 0–4–4Ts were of considerable interest. In 1883 they can be presumed to have been all green with numbers on the boiler side as at *Plate 1*. It may equally well be presumed that some of them probably became red when first fitted with Johnson cabs if they weren't already (cabs were fitted from 1889 onwards). It is certain that most of them at this time also had their brass numerals moved from boiler side to cab panel, but still with no indication of ownership on the bunker side (*Plate 7*). Soon afterwards, the normal Johnson livery exemplified by Nos. 786 and 692A (*Plates 2 & 3*) became customary. We are, however, unable to see why some of them retained works plates (seemingly the Beyer-Peacock series) and others lost them (again, seemingly the Dübs engines). The pioneer engine, No. 690/690A, later No. 1200, had its own peculiar variation (*Plates 8 & 9*), but it may not have been alone in this respect.

We have no positive evidence to suggest any overtly 'decorated' liveries of the 'Kentish Town' school were applied to these engines in the late 19th century and this may perhaps seem surprising in view of the treatment given at the same time to humble 0–6–0Ts (see, for example Volume One, *Plates 224-6*). Again, we would welcome details from readers who know of any such evidence.

The advent of the simplified Deeley crimson livery with its large transfer numerals posed something of a problem with the Kirtley 0–4–4Ts. The side panel ahead of the cab door was decreed too small for customary procedure to be followed, so the numerals, generally of 14 in size, went to the tank bunker side. The engines remained otherwise anonymous (as was the custom with most Midland tank engines in Deeley's time and afterwards) save for the MR on the buffer plank and on the works plates. *Plate 11* shows the normal treatment at this time but one or two (e.g. *Plate 10*) received the 18 in. figures and looked distinctly peculiar with them.

Regardless of livery (Johnson or Deeley), it seems clear that only the Beyer-Peacock engines sported brass splasher beading, and this feature seems to have been emphasised both before and after the livery change – compare, for example. *Plates 3 & 11*. In time, however, even the Beyer-Peacock engines had the splasher beading 'over-painted'.

The LMS was quite prepared to run the engines for another ten years (more, in some cases) and we shall cover this part of the story in our companion work*. However, to round out the picture, *Plates 12 & 6* show examples of these wonderfully quaint old engines in their two most typical LMS period configurations.

**Illustrated History of LMS Locomotives, Vol. 4.*

Plate 2. No. 786 was built by Dübs & Co. in 1870 and compared with *Plate 3* shows the flared top to the bunker and footplate angle iron which differed from those of the Beyer Peacock locomotives. Note also the different condenser pipe arrangement and the changed position of the ascending step below the cab opening. Seen here at Kentish Town in full crimson lake livery, the engine, compared with *Plate 3* shows lining just below the cabroof and a bright finish to the condensing pipe along the side of the boiler. The picture is clearly of earlier vintage. Becoming No. 1212 in 1907, this locomotive was withdrawn in 1921, the only pre-LMS period casualty.
Authors' Collection

Plate 3. No. 692A c.1904. Built in 1869 by Beyer Peacock and renumbered on the duplicate list in 1898, this locomotive was to become No. 1202 in 1907 and was withdrawn by the LMS in 1928. The lining details are interesting in so far that although full lining is evident above the platform, the lining below is sparse and appears to be only on the outside cranks and on the wheels. *Authors' Collection*

Plates 4 & 5 (opposite). Beyer Peacock-built No. 1205 (ex-No. 695A) and Dübs-built No. 1221 (ex-No. 795) show the Deeley modifications to the two series of Kirtley 0—4—4Ts, both displaying curved front handrails. Both engines are in Deeley simplified crimson livery and No. 1205, additionally, has had the condensing apparatus removed. It also displays straight 'levers' to the Salter safety valves (somewhat obscured against the chimney in the background). This was somewhat unusual for this class in their Johnson (and later) condition — see other views.

Authors' Collection

Plate 6. No. 1219 is seen here at Kentish Town in what seems to be LMS post-1928 plain black livery. We can see no trace of any red lining although some Kirtley 0–4–4Ts did get the lined black style. Note the change in smokebox door (c.f. *Plates 4 & 5*) but the retention of condensing gear. Originally No. 793, this locomotive was the final survivor of the class, being withdrawn at the end of 1935.

Authors' Collection

Plate 7. Dübs-built No. 797 (later no. 1223) shows an example of Kirtley 0–4–4T carrying the early crimson livery (with its number now on the cab panel – c.f. *Plate 1*) but before the adoption of the letters 'MR'. The works plate between the two coupled wheel axle-boxes reads 'Rebuilt Derby 1890' so the picture must have been taken some time between 1890 and c.1892 (when 'MR' was first applied to locomotive side panels).
Authors' Collection

Plate 8. This interesting rear view of No. 690A shows the pioneer Kirtley 0–4–4T with its own particular version of insignia layout (running number between 'M' and 'R'), probably in the early 1900s. There seems to be little lining to speak of below the running plate (similar in fact to *Plate 3*) and it seems likely that this treatment exemplifies the gradual move to simplicity of the earlier Deeley period, immediately preceding the new livery and re-numbering of 1905-7. This engine almost certainly retained this precise livery when first renumbered (see *Plate 9*).
Authors' Collection

Plate 9. No. 690A is here seen as No. 1200 in St. Pancras carrying its new 1907 number which has been applied by using brass numerals without change of livery from the condition shown at *Plate 8*. Note also the flat Deeley smokebox door. Whilst the engine is fully lined above the platform, only the outside cranks appear to be lined below footplate level. *Collection Bernard Mathews*

Plate 10. No. 1206 at Malvern Wells in September 1917 depicts a locomotive in simplified crimson lake livery with 18in high running numbers. Originally No. 780, this locomotive lasted until 1928 when it was withdrawn from service. *Collection Roger Carpenter*

Plate 11. No. 1204 in simplified crimson lake livery. Note the brass beading on the splashers (believed confined to the Beyer Peacock series) and flat Deeley smokebox door. Only the outside cranks and wheel tyres are lined below platform level. Originally No. 694, this locomotive lasted until 1928. *Collection Bernard Mathews*

Plate 12. No. 1208 was originally No. 782, later 782A (1898-1907). Photographed at St. Pancras in the LMS pre-1928 period, the engine, LMS markings excepted, is still in simplified Deeley livery. The reader's attention is directed to the front lamp iron positions, particularly clearly shown in this view and characteristic of the class. Note also the dished smokebox door but original handrail arrangement when compared with No. 1219 seen in *Plate 6*. No. 1208 was withdrawn from service in 1930. *Collection Bernard Mathews*

Plate 13. '6' class 0–4–4T No. 18 (later No. 1228) is shown in this view more or less as it would have been during the 1880s, with built-up chimney and fitted with condensing apparatus. However, the 'MR' on the tank side and closed cab suggest a later 1890s date for the picture. Note the front toolbox, later changed for the style shown at *Plate 23*, but whose presence was always characteristic of this first group of Johnson 0–4–4Ts.
Authors' Collection

THE JOHNSON 0-4-4T CLASSES

The Johnson 0–4–4Ts eventually numbered 205 examples (1907 Nos. 1226-1430) and, superficially, they were all very similar in appearance. However, like his 2–4–0s and 4–4–0s, there were small differences between the various series albeit that they all shared very constant visual lines. As usual, therefore, it was not immediately apparent at first glance which series was which. Therefore, before analysing them in detail, it seems helpful to give a basic summary of the whole group. As usual, the Midland differentiated them by individual class designation based on the first running number principle and the summary at Table 1 reflects this fact. Unless stated otherwise, it may safely be assumed that the anatomical and livery changes to be described applied across the board as it were.

The basic Johnson 0–4–4T first appeared in 1875 with the building of the '6' class, all displaying open footplate and rear weatherboards, somewhat in the Kirtley manner, but this configuration was changed in due course to the 'closed' cab style. It was in this form that most of the Johnson engines first appeared, the exceptions being some of the condensing engines, and as far as the 'red engine' period is concerned, *all* Johnson 0–4–4Ts became 'closed cab' engines.

The '6' class (*Plate 13*) was a small group of but ten engines with 5 ft 3 in drivers, all originally fitted with condensers. After removal of condensing gear, these were most readily distinguished, at first glance, by the front toolboxes on each side, outboard of the leading splashers. These engines were speedily followed into service by a closed cab non-condensing variation with larger driving wheels 5 ft 6½ in diameter. This was the '1252' class of which 30 were eventually built (*Plate 14*) originally without bunker coal rails, but basically setting the style for all subsequent Johnson 0–4–4Ts.

There then followed a break in construction of some five years, during which time the Midland seems to have decided that the smaller driving wheel was preferable, and all subsequent 0–4–4Ts had 5 ft 3½ in, demonstrating yet again the obsessive MR concern for the odd half inch. This later series of engines became what most people regard as the 'definitive' Johnson 0–4–4T and all the various sub-classes (Table 1) were very similar in appearance. There was

Plate 14. No. 1279 (later No. 1253) was one of many 0–4–4Ts whose pre- and post-1907 numbers were so close as to cause some confusion of identity. As shown here, it represents the '1252' class as built with closed cab and no coal rails on the bunker. The view is probably 'ex-works' (Neilson & Co.) and the livery is unquestionably green. Note the wooden brake blocks. *Authors' Collection*

a gradual increase in cylinder dimensions and/or boiler pressure through the series, plus a slight extension of bogie wheelbase from 5 ft to 5 ft 6 in from the '1532' class onwards; but the principal visual differences, livery apart, were represented either by condensing apparatus, if fitted, or bunker shape. Some examples displayed both together. At *Plates 15-18* the four basic classes are shown and *Plates 19-22* show the condenser and bunker variations.

In terms of livery, the whole of the '6' class and '1252' class came into service painted dark green with the earlier examples of the '1532' class in light green. As far as we can deduce, the first five condensing engines of this series (Nos. 1547-51, later Nos. 1281-5 were green (built in 1882), together with the five 1883-built engines (Nos. 1632-6, later Nos. 1286-90) which entered service before the change to Crimson Lake was made. Indeed it is recorded that No. 1636 was the last new locomotive to enter service in the light green livery.

The rest of the Johnson 0–4–4Ts were built from 1884 through to 1900 and were painted red from the beginning. At first, and probably up to the end of the 2218 series (No. 2227, later No. 1380) this is likely to have been without 'MR' lettering and with fairly simple lining. However, the *condensing* engines of 1886, mostly seem to have been given much more elaborate lining – see page 19, also *Plate 19*. The final '2228' class series with extended bunkers probably carried 'MR' from new and slightly more lining as 'standard'. Other livery variations (including Deeley styles) are given in the class summaries.

Structurally, the 0–4–4Ts went through the typical Deeley/Fowler 'front end' modifications from the early 20th century onwards, but with little really significant change in basic engine shape. However, from the 1920s onwards, some of them were given replacement Belpaire boilers, and this *did* change their looks, e.g. *Plate 22*. So, too, did the LMS fitting of motor train control gear and the changing of livery to lined black. The picture coverage in this chapter gives some examples of these latter-day alterations but, for the most part, the LMS continuation will be found in our companion LMS History, thus allowing more MR period views in this book.

The Johnson 0–4–4Ts were, in their way, as characteristic of the Midland as any type we can think of. They were almost everywhere on the system and for this reason we have tried to give a very extensive picture coverage of the type in the detailed summaries which follow. No serious modeller of the Midland should be without one and we hope we have given him (or her) plenty of choice!

Plate 15. 0—4—4T No. 1539 (later No. 1273) is an early, non-condensing example of the '1532' class, more or less 'as built'. The picture is undated so the engine could have been green or red, given the lack of 'MR' on the tank side and the original 'Derby 1881' works plate on the bunker. Such lining as can be detected (via a magnifying glass on the original picture!) tempts us to think it is an early form of the red livery.
Authors' Collection

Plate 16. This member of the '1823' class (i.e. '1532' class built with 18in x 24in cylinders) was one of a relatively small batch of engines built in 1889 and 1892. The view shows No. 1348 (originally No. 1429) at Sheffield around the 1910-15 period. Deeley front end excepted, the most obvious difference from the '1532' class example at *Plate 15* is probably the livery – now the Deeley simplified style.
Collection Bernard Mathews

Plate 17. This fascinating view, taken at Leeds c.1905, shows a member of the '1833' class in final Johnson livery but with new Deeley style smokebox door and numberplate, yet original Johnson chimney and handrail. Whilst not unique, this particular combination of features was not particularly common and would only be seen for a year or so c.1905-8. The engine, No. 1841, became No. 1359 in 1907. *J. H. Wright*

Plate 18. The slightly longer bunker of the '2228' class is shown in this view of No. 2627 (later No. 1427), one of the last few Johnson 0—4—4Ts to be built, in 1900. The tank/bunker sides were also marginally deeper in this final series of engines. The livery, although somewhat obscured by grime in this view, reveals itself (under magnification) to be undiluted turn of the century 'Johnson', as would be expected. *Authors' Collection*

Plate 19. No. 1718 (later No. 1311) with modified bunker shape, was also the first condenser fitted example in the 1385 batch of the '1532' class – see also page 24. The livery is the very elaborate 'London' style of the later 1890s, clearly apparent even though the picture is not of prime quality. There appears to be lining on just about every conceivable visible surface. *Authors' Collection*

Plates 20 & 21 (overleaf). The condenser fitted examples of the '1833' and '2228' classes (see also pages 28 & 30) were otherwise no different from the non-condensing members of the two classes and retained the normal bunker shape. This is clearly shown on Nos. 2224 (later No. 1377) and 2229 (later No. 1382). However, the somewhat similar angle of view clearly makes apparent the longer bunker and slightly deeper tank and bunker sides of the later type (No. 2229). Both engines carry the early 20th century Johnson livery (c.1900-3 we guess). *Authors' Collection*

Plate 22. This early LMS view of '1833' class 0–4–4T No. 1373 (originally No. 2220), shows a condenser fitted engine also carrying the new G5½ Belpaire boiler, fitted to some engines from the 1920s onwards. The 'front end' carries all the normal post-Johnson changes.
Authors' Collection

6 CLASS

(Sometimes referred to as 'Class C')

Summary

Built at Derby 1875.
Originally Midland Railway numbers 6, 15, 18, 137, 140-144, 147.
Midland Railway 1907 numbers 1226-1235, all to LMS.
Class extinct 1935.
Originally built with open footplate and rear weatherboard but were later rebuilt with enclosed cabs as shown in the diagram. Condenser-fitted originally.

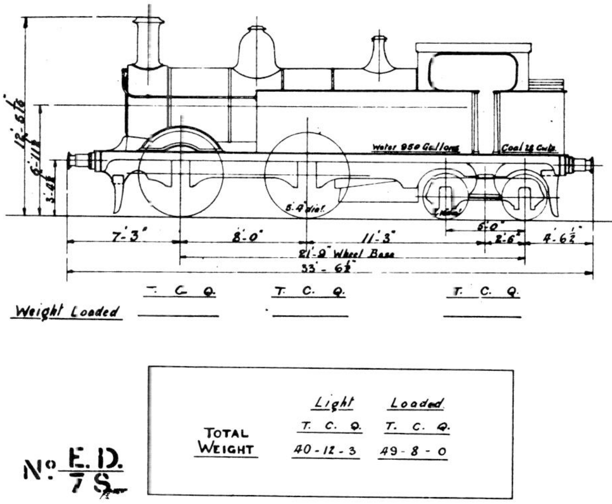

Fig. 2. This Engine Diagram was the 1910 Midland Railway diagram issued for the '6' class of locomotives.
Authors' Collection

Plate 23. No. 142 after transfer on loan to the M & GNR. One of three locomotives exchanged for four M & GN 4–4–0Ts, the locomotive is in simplified crimson lake livery with M & GNR identification and has been fitted with tablet exchange apparatus. Note the newer type toolboxes, one each side of the locomotive (see *Plate 13*). No. 142 became No. 1232 in 1907 and was withdrawn from service in 1926.
National Railway Museum

Plate 24. No. 1234 in LMS pre-1928 crimson lake livery. Originally No. 144, this locomotive was to be withdrawn in 1930. The two coal rails on the bunker were normal policy for this class, but less common than the three rails of later series. *Collection Bernard Mathews*

Plate 25. Pioneer Johnson 0–4–4T No. 6 was withdrawn in 1930 for possible preservation. It was, of course, carrying No. 1226 at the time. For a year or two it lay at Derby Works restored to a spurious Johnson livery, yet retaining all its post-Johnson changes. It is seen thus in this picture. Sadly, Stanier had it broken up in 1932, ironically the very same year that the last Derby 0–4–4T (the LMS standard type) was built. It is a great shame that the engine was not kept. It was a design which gave more than 75 years of valuable service to MR, LMS and BR in turn and far more typical than many preserved engines – but then, perhaps we are biased! *Authors' Collection*

1252 CLASS

Summary

Built by Neilson & Co. 1875/6.
Originally Midland Railway numbers 1262-1274, 1275-1279, 1280/1, 1252-1261.
Midland Railway 1907 numbers 1236-1265, all except No. 1245 to LMS.
Some renumbered in the 580XX series by British Railways following nationalisation.
Some motor-fitted by the Midland Railway and the LMS.
Class extinct 1954.

No. 1262 was the first locomotive to be built and some sources refer to this class as the 1262 class. We have adopted the policy of using the lowest number of the series built, hence 1252 as recorded above. When built they were not vacuum fitted (see *Plate 14*).

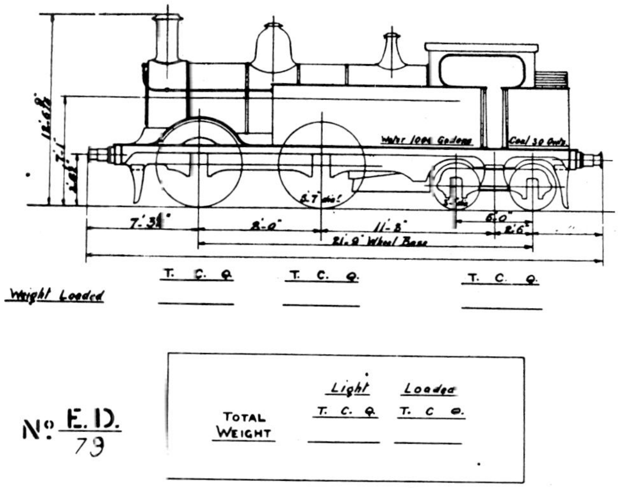

Fig. 3. Engine Diagram 79 was the 1910 Midland Railway diagram for the old '1252' class which by that date had been renumbered as noted. *Authors' Collection*

Plate 26. We believe this picture illustrates new No. 1262 which was originally old No. 1258 and is seen here in simplified crimson lake livery with no lining below the footplate platform. All the boiler lagging bands are lined and the engine retains its old handrail. However, there has to be a possibility that it could be old No. 1262 which was to become new No. 1236 in 1907. New No. 1262 was withdrawn in 1934 while new No. 1236's service ended in 1930. *Collection A. G. Ellis*

Plate 27. No. 1247 in LMS post-1928 intermediate passenger livery, black with red lining. Originally No. 1273, it was to last until the end of 1949 and, although allocated the number 58032 by British Railways, it did not carry this number before withdrawal. Note the three coal rails on the bunker (see *Plate 24*).
Collection V. Forster

Plate 28. No. 1239 is seen here as motor-fitted by the LMS and carrying LMS 1928 intermediate passenger livery. No. 1239 was originally No. 1265 and was withdrawn in 1949 before carrying its British Railways number which would have been 58030.
Collection V. R. Anderson

Plate 29. A number of locomotives carried British Railways numbers and were equipped with Belpaire boilers. BR No. 58036, originally built as No. 1281, was one such example. Becoming No. 1255 in 1907, it was to last until 1950 and is seen here at Burton about four weeks prior to its withdrawal from service, still carrying LMS on the side tanks and in motor-fitted condition.
W. L. Good

1532 CLASS

Summary

Built at Derby 1881-1886.
Original Midland Railway numbers 1532-1551, 1632-1656, 1718-1737.
Midland Railway 1907 numbers 1266-1330, all but Nos. 1281-2 to LMS (No. 1305 ex-S & DJR in 1930).
Some renumbered in the 580XX series by British Railways following Nationalisation.
Class extinct 1956.
Note: Nos. 1547-1551 (1281-1285) and 1718-1722 (1311-1315) were condenser fitted when built and Nos. 1723-8 (1316-21) were condenser fitted soon afterwards.
Many received Belpaire boilers from the mid-1920s and a number were motor-fitted by the LMS.

The '1532' class, the first of the 0–4–4Ts with the 5 ft 6 in wheelbase bogie, showed two distinct visual variations, depending on whether or not they were fitted with condensing apparatus. Those which were, eventually 16 in total, were all given flared top bunkers with auxiliary coal rails. Additionally, it would seem that at least the *second* series of condenser-fitted engines (Nos. 1718-28, later Nos. 1311-21) all carried elaborately lined liveries from a very early date, certainly before 'MR' appeared on the tank side (*Plate 35*). This elaboration continued through the 1890s after the introduction of 'MR' and seems to have been unique to this group. We have found no evidence to suggest Nos. 1547-51 (later No. 1281-5) were similarly finished – but they may have been. The non-condensing engines of the class do not seem to have been given 'special' Johnson liveries over and above standard practices for the period in question.

In the interests of better understanding, we have split the pictorial review of this class into the two basic types, starting with the non-condensing engines.

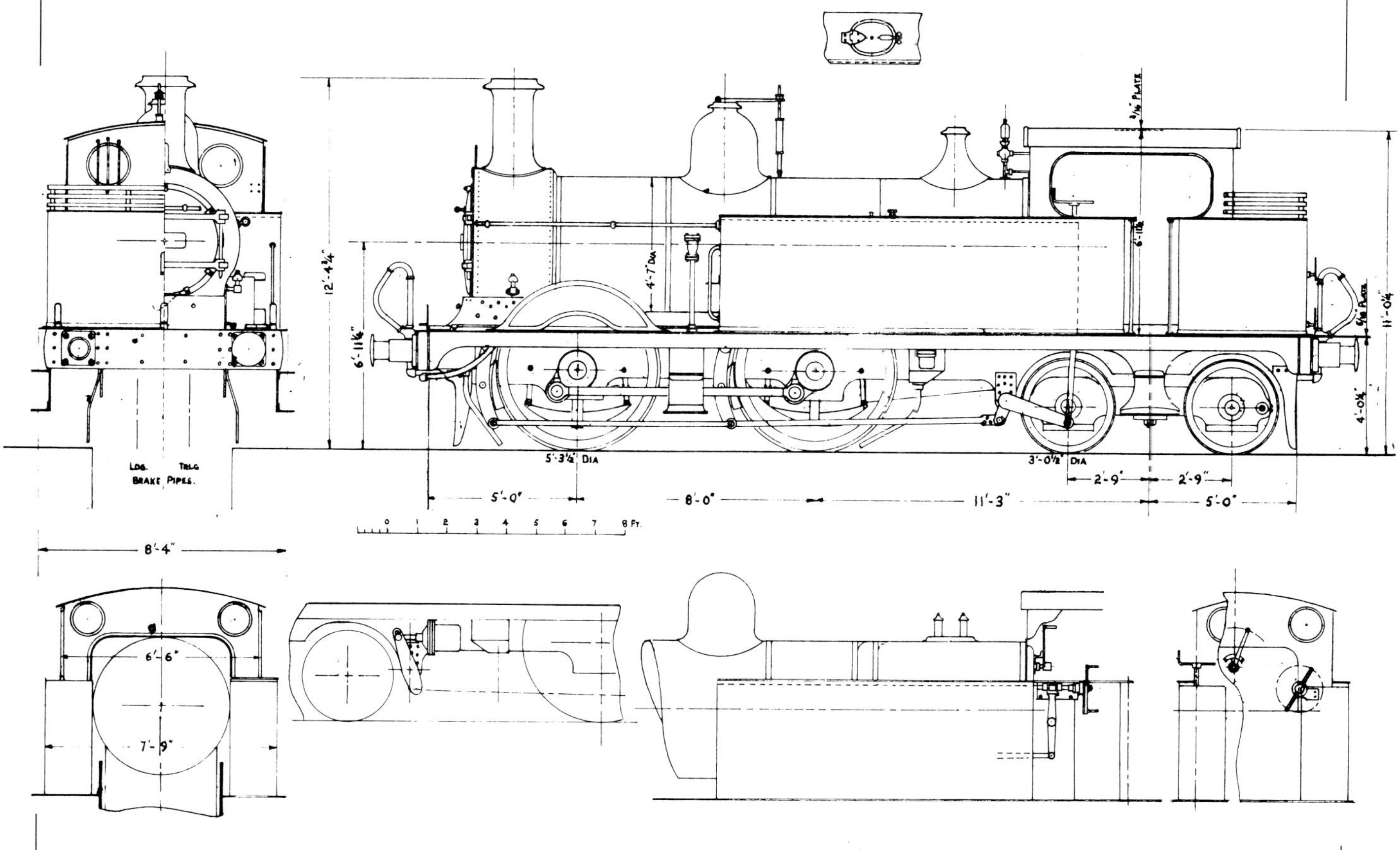

Fig. 4. When in non-condensing condition, the '1532' class were, in 1910, allocated by the Midland Railway to Engine Diagram 80, but we have chosen, instead, to use this excellent Ken Woodhead drawing to illustrate the type in its later stage. The drawing is also accurate for the '1823' class, 1907 Nos. 1331-50, which only differed in cylinder size. It is also virtually accurate for the non-condensing engines of the '1833' class, 1907 Nos. 1351-70. K. C. Woodhead

Plates 30 & 31 (opposite). These two excellent views show opposite sides of the non-condensing '1532' class. Both are taken after 1892 as the 'MR' is present on the tank side; but the view of No. 1636 (later No. 1290) could well be anything between five and ten years earlier than that of No. 1546 (later No. 1280). Not only does No. 1636 still possess a 'built-up' chimney, but it also lacks lining on guard irons and brake hangers and the front ascending steps have not been added just ahead of the tank side. These features seem to have started to appear shortly after the adoption of 'MR' lettering in the mid-1890s and are clearly shown on No. 1546, a slightly older engine. We reckon the pictures to be c.1893 and c.1905 respectively. The big clerestory coaches in the background behind No. 1546 suggest an earliest possible date of 1898-1900, but we prefer c.1905. Both pictures were taken in Yorkshire, at Manningham (No. 1636) and Leeds Wellington (No. 1546) and between them show the subtle but definite changes which took place in Midland locomotive decoration during the 1890s and early 1900s and upon which we elaborated in detail in Volume One.

Roger Carpenter and J. H. Wright

1532 CLASS – CONVENTIONAL, NON-CONDENSING

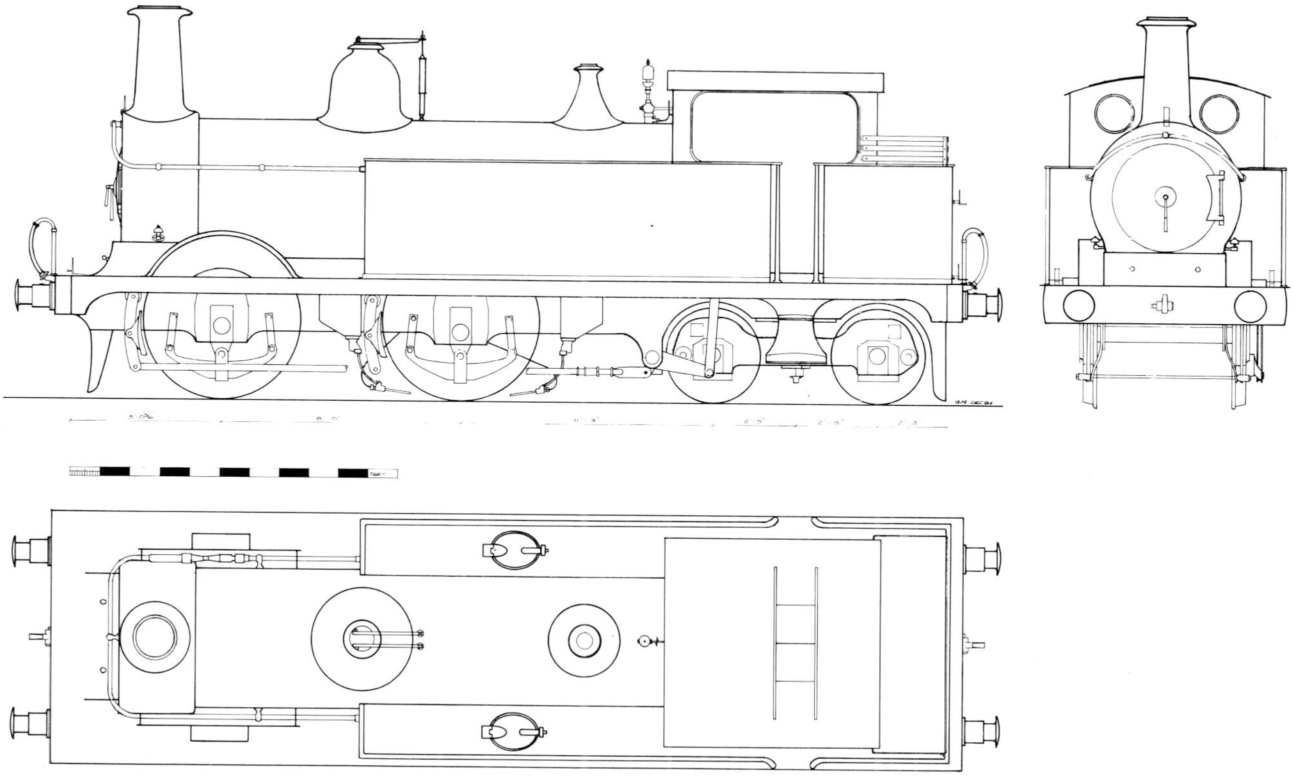

Fig. 5. This drawing by Geoff Goodfellow depicts the series which became Nos. 1331-1370 in 1907. The drawing shows the locomotive in Johnson condition and, when used with Fig. 4, it is possible to build any of the non-condensing locomotives from the series, whose numbers were 1266-1370. Readers should note the altered sandbox positions of the later series when compared with the earlier locomotives.

G. Goodfellow

Plate 32. No. 1277 in simplified crimson lake livery without any evidence of yellow lining on the wheel tyres. Built as No. 1543 and becoming No. 1277 in 1907, this locomotive was withdrawn by the LMS in 1946. Note the full 'front end' changes compared with *Plates 30/31.* *Collection Bernard Mathews*

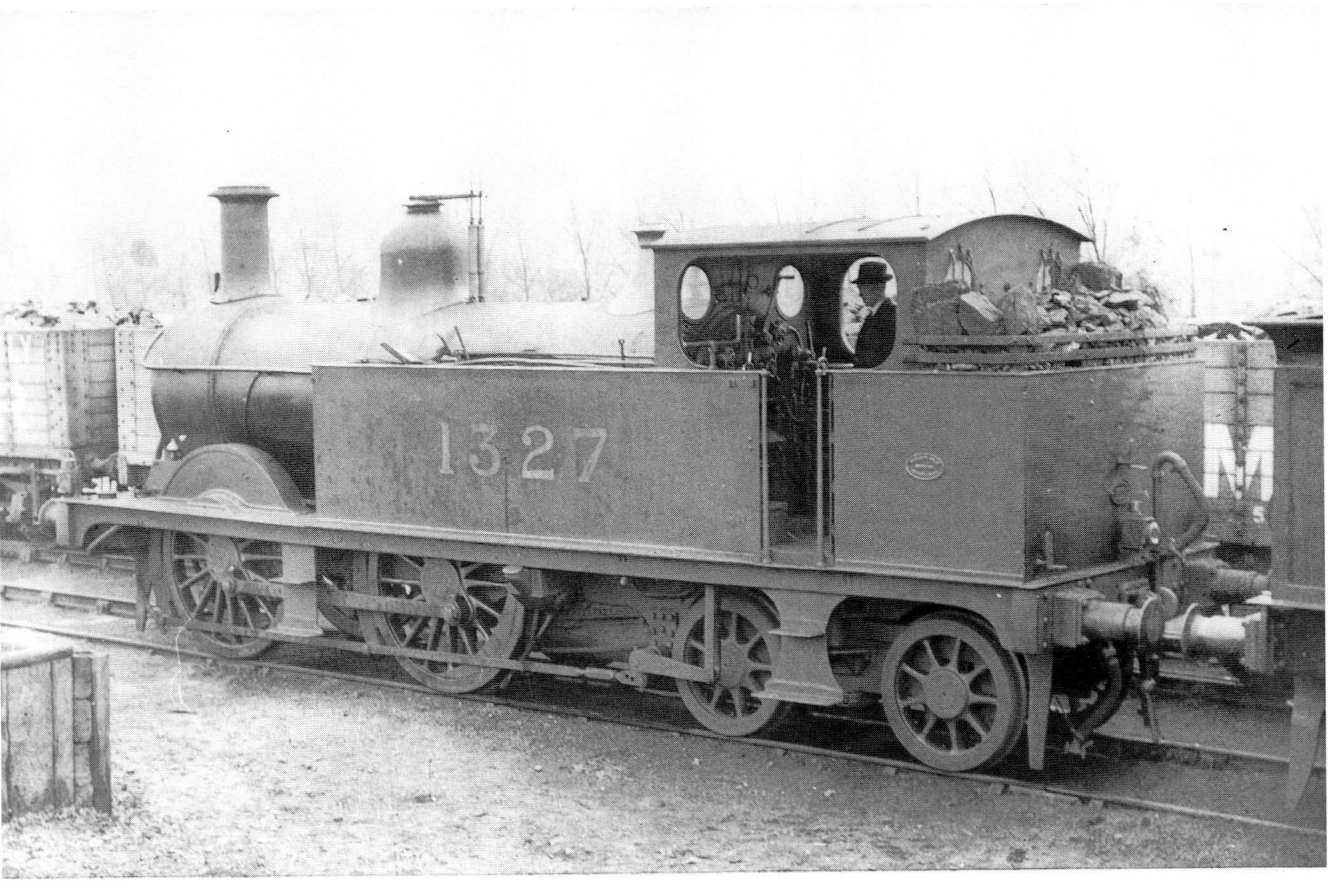

Plate 33. No. 1327, photographed at Bournville in April 1922, displays the simplified Deeley crimson lake livery in rather scruffy condition. Apart from providing a good view of the bunker rear, it also shows the cab roof ventilator arrangement which is more fully described on page 70 of Volume One. Originally No. 1734, this locomotive lasted until withdrawal by the LMS in 1940. Note, c.f. *Plates 24/27*, that this engine, unusually, has but two coal rails on the bunker. *W. L. Good*

Plate 34. In immaculate LMS post-1928 black livery (there is little evidence of red lining although it must surely have been there), this engine is a motor-fitted locomotive running with a round-top C class boiler. The motor-fitting was an LMS modification. Originally No. 1539, No. 1273 was renumbered 58040 by British Railways and as such lasted until withdrawal in 1955.

Collection B. Mathews

1532 CLASS – CONDENSER-FITTED

Plate 35. This view of 0–4–4T No. 1722 (later No. 1315) clearly shows that the condenser-fitted engines of the '1532' class were given their elaborate liveries at an early stage. There is no 'MR' on the tank side and the chimney is the original 'built-up', so the date of the picture is somewhere between the date of build (1886) and the introduction of 'MR' (1892). The extra lining, especially on tank front, is quite clear and there is a plethora of extra lining on spring hangers and guard irons. This treatment, therefore, was well ahead of the similar moves on the tender engines (see Vol. 1) and we are inclined to think that these condensing 0–4–4Ts were probably the first MR engines to receive 'decorated' liveries. *Authors' Collection*

Plate 36. No 1725 shows another condenser-fitted 0–4–4T in fully decorated crimson lake livery, this time with 'MR'. Note the outward flare to the bunker to be found on all the condenser fitted locomotives of the '1532' class. A third view of this treatment is at *Plate 19*. Note the lining on the tank and bunker sides, edged black and fine lined yellow with large round-cornered panels comprising a black band fine-lined yellow on both sides. No. 1725 became No. 1318 in 1907 and was withdrawn from service in 1930. *Authors' Collection*

Plates 37 & 38. Condensing 0–4–4T No. 1285 in Midland and LMS livery. Compare the smokebox doors. Both are dished but with altered handrail arrangement. On the LMS locomotive the front sanding arrangement for the control gear has been altered when compared with the Midland locomotive. The latter is in simplified crimson lake livery with brass beading to the splasher whereas the LMS locomotive was probably in lined black livery although very dirty. No. 1285 was originally No. 1551 and was withdrawn at the end of 1931.

Collection Bernard Mathews

Plate 39. No. 1316 in simplified crimson lake livery and rather disgracefully dirty in its final Midland Railway years. Originally No. 1723, it was to last until 1925 and as such was one of the early withdrawals of this class. This excellent broadside view shows very clearly the revised bunker shape of these condenser-fitted engines.

Collection Roger Carpenter

Fig. 6. Engine Diagram 83 was the 1910 Midland diagram for the condenser-fitted 0–4–4Ts Nos. 1371-1380 but actually shows the bunker shape for the '1833' class non-condenser engines, hence its inclusion at this point. *National Railway Museum*

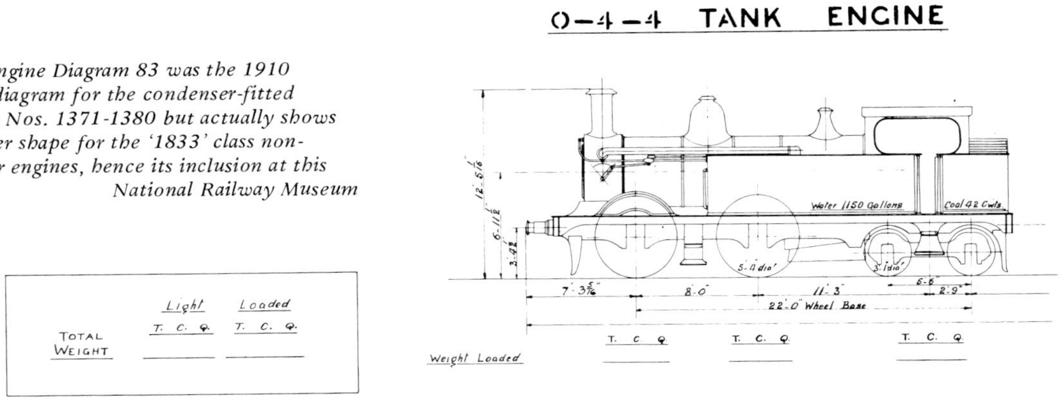

1823 AND 1833 CLASSES

Summary

(a) 1823 CLASS

Built at Derby 1889-1892.

Original Midland Railway numbers 1823-1832, 1322-1326, 202, 1428-1430, 1697.

Midland Railway 1907 numbers 1331-1350, all to LMS.

(b) 1833 CLASS

Built by Dübs & Co., 1892 and Neilson 1893.

Original Midland Railway numbers 1833-1842, 2013-2022, 2218-2227.

Midland Railway 1907 numbers 1351-1380, all to LMS.

Many received Belpaire boilers from the mid-1920s and a number were motor-fitted by the LMS.

When both these classes were built they were visually identical to the non-condensing '1532' class (see *Fig. 5*), and were all put on engine diagram 80. Some were renumbered in the 580XX series by British Railways following Nationalisation. The essential differences were that the '1823' class had larger cylinders than the '1532' class when they were built and the '1833' class had higher boiler pressure as well. Both types were extinct in 1959.

As with the preceding '1532' class, some of these engines (all from the '1833' class) were given condensing apparatus from new but *without* the bunker modifications of the '1532' series. These were Nos. 2218-27, later Nos. 1371-80. They were later allocated to engine diagram 81 in this form (*Fig. 6*) and we have separated them for analysis.

Plate 40. '1823' class 0–4–4T No. 1334 carrying an LMS 22C shed code. The former 'MR' pattern shed plate has been removed and 22C painted onto the smokebox door c.1935. This locomotive was originally No. 1826 and is seen here when fitted with a Belpaire boiler and in LMS (lined?) black! No. 1334 remained in service until 1946.
Collection Bernard Mathews

Plate 41. '1833' class 0–4–4T No. 1366 in LMS lined black post-1928 livery. The red lining is very faint, however. This locomotive was originally No. 2018 and lasted until 1950 and was withdrawn still carrying its 1907 Midland, later LMS, number. Its allocated British Railways number was 58064.
Authors' Collection

Plate 42. '1833' class No. M1365 displays the first British Railways livery style prior to the establishment of the renumbering scheme which saw the addition of 40000 to the numbers of most, but not all, ex-LMS locomotives. The 0–4–4Ts, amongst other pre-group locomotives, were eventually to be allocated numbers in the 58XXX series. Built as No. 2017, No. 1365 was allocated the number 58063 but was scrapped in 1951 without ever being renumbered. When photographed at Ashchurch in May 1948, M1365 had received a Belpaire boiler.
W. L. Good

Plate 43. No. 2017 was a Dübs-built engine, built in 1892 and due to become No. 1365 in 1907. In its final years we illustrate it as M1365 at *Plate 42.* *Authors' Collection*

Plate 44. Condensing No. 1374 is seen here carrying simplified Deeley livery. Built as No. 2221, it became No. 1374 in 1907 and was scrapped in 1946. This clear broadside view makes an interesting comparison with *Plate 39*, clearly showing the difference between the bunkers of the two condensing series. *Authors' Collection*

Plate 45. Condensing '1833' class No. 1375 is seen at Derby in LMS post-1928 intermediate passenger livery, black with red lining. Note the rounded corners – when lined in red livery the panels had square corners. Note also that the spectacle plates frames have been polished. Built as No. 2222, this locomotive became No. 1375 in 1907 and received a Belpaire boiler in the mid-1920s. It was renumbered 58070 by British Railways and was withdrawn from service in 1953. *Authors' Collection*

TABLE 1 – THE KIRTLEY AND JOHNSON 0-4-4T CLASSES

1903 Diagram Page No.	Order No. or Class	Built by	Quantity Built	Date of Building	Pre 1907 Numbers	1907 Numbers	Cylinders	BOILER Centre Line	BOILER Diameter	BOILER Length	BOILER Tubes	BOILER Diameter	Working Pressure	FIREBOX Length	FIREBOX Grate Area in Sq Ft	Total Heating Surface in Sq Ft	WHEELS Coupled	WHEELS Bogie	WHEELS Tyres	ENGINE WEIGHT Empty	ENGINE WEIGHT Loaded	Water Capacity in Gallons	Coal in CWTs	REMARKS
62	Beyers	Beyer Peacock	6	1869	690A-695A	1200-1205	18″ × 24″	6′8″	4′2″	10′6″	246	1⅝″	140 PSI	5′6″	16	1255	5′2½″	3′0½″	2¾″	not quoted	not quoted	1000	39	Originally 690-695 known as 690 class.
33	Dübs Condensers	Dübs	20	1870	780-799	1206-1225	18″ × 24″	6′7½″	4′2″	10′6″	246	1⅝″	140 PSI	5′6″	16	1255	5′2½″	3′0½″	2¾″		48.18.1	1000	39	Nos 780-783 became 780A-783A in 1898 and were allocated page 63 in the 1903 Diagram Book just because they were duplicated stock. Known as 780 class. Originally 17″ × 24″ cyls.
THE JOHNSON BUILT ENGINES																								
35	1*	Derby	10	1875	6, 15, 18, 137, 140-4, 147	1226-1235	17″ × 24″	6′11″	4′2″	10′6″	236	1⅝″	140 PSI	5′6″	16	1209	5′3½″	2′9½″	2¾″	39.10.1	48.9.7	950	Not Quoted	Originally built with open cabs. Some to 18″ × 24″ cyls by 1903. Known as 6 class. Condenser fitted.
34	D	Neilsons	30	1875/6	1252-1281	1236-1265	17″ × 24″	7′0½″	4′2″	10′6″	246	1⅝″	140 PSI	5′6″	16	1254	5′6½″	3′0½″	2¾″	40.3.1	47.17.2	1000	Not Quoted	Known as 1252 class. Note that although both number blocks are continuous, they did NOT correlate in number order. Most with 18″ × 24″ cyls by July 1903.
32	289	Derby	20	1881/2	1532-1551	1266-1285	18″ × 24″	6′11¼″	4′2″	10′6″	246	1⅝″	140 PSI	5′6″	16	1254	5′3½″	3′0½″	2¾″	40.11.3	50.9.7	1150	42	Known as 1532 class. 1547-1551 condensing. Weights for empty 41.14.1, loaded 50.17.2. All condenser fitted engines worked the Metropolitan Line traffic. All built with 17″ × 24″ cycls. Later altered to 18″ × 24″.
	415		5	1883	1632-1636	1286-1290																		
	460		20	1883/4	1637-1656	1291-1310																		
	538		10	1885	1718-1727	1311-1320																		All condenser fitted.
	589		10	1886	1728-1737	1321-1330																		1728 condenser fitted.
	763		10	1889	1823-1832	1331-1340																		Some sources refer to o/n 763 as 1823 class. Built with 18″ × 24″ cyls.
31	K	Dübs	20	1892	1833-1842 2013-2022	1351-1360 1361-1370	18″ × 24″	6′11¼″	4′2″	10′6″	246	1⅝″	150 PSI	5′6″	16	1254	5′3½″	3′0½″	2¾″	40.11.3	50.9.7	1150	42	Notwithstanding the Midland Railway Diagram page allocations, some sources refer to these locomotives as the 1823 class.
	981		10	1892	1322-1326, 202, 1428-30, 1697	1341-1350							140 PSI											
30	P	Neilsons	10	1893	2218-2227	1371-1380	18″ × 24″	6′11¼″	4′2″	10′6″	244	1⅝″	150 PSI	5′6″	16	1246	5′3½″	3′0½″	2¾″	41.14.4	50.17.2	1150	42	Some sources refer to these as the 1823 class. All condenser fitted.
29	K2/94	Dübs	15	1895	2233-2247	1386-1400	18″ × 24″	7′3″	4′2″	10′6″	244	1⅝″	150 PSI	5′6″	16	1252	5′3½″	3′0½″	2¾″	40.18.3	51.18.3	1270	42	Some sources refer to the series which became 1381-1430 as the 2228 class.
	1602	Derby	10	1898	690-695 780-783	1401-1406 1407-1410																		
28	K2/99	Dübs	20	1900	2611-2630	1411-1430	18″ × 24″	7′3¼″	4′2″	10′6″	244	1⅝″	150 PSI	5′6″	16	1252	5′4″	3′1″	3″	42.8.3	53.10.1	1270	42	See above re class designation.
27	P2	Dübs	5	1895	2228-2232	1381-1385	18″ × 24″	7′3″	4′2″	10′6″	244	1⅝″	150 PSI	5′6″	16	1252	5′3½″	3′0½″	2¾″	41.16.2	51.12.0	1270	42	Built with condensers. Removed 8/02 from 2228/9/30. 2228 class.

*According to Radford, *'Derby Works & Midland Locomotives'*, they were known as Class C, the only example of a Derby built class being given a 'letter designation' rather than an order No. However, the 1903 Midland Diagram Book quotes o/n 1 for this series and Class C for the Beyer 4-4-0's Nos 2581-2590.

Principal source 1903 Midland Railway Diagram Book.

2228 CLASS

Summary

Built by Dübs & Co. 1895.
Original Midland Railway numbers 2228-2247.
Built at Derby 1898.
Original Midland Railways numbers 690-695, 780-783.
Built by Dübs & Co. 1900
Original Midland Railway numbers 2611-2630.
Midland Railway 1907 numbers 1381-1430, all to LMS.

Similar to 1833 class but with longer bunkers and slightly deeper tanks. Some were renumbered in the 580XX series by British Railways following Nationalisation.
Many received Belpaire boilers from the mid-1920s and some were motor-fitted by the LMS.
Class extinct 1960.

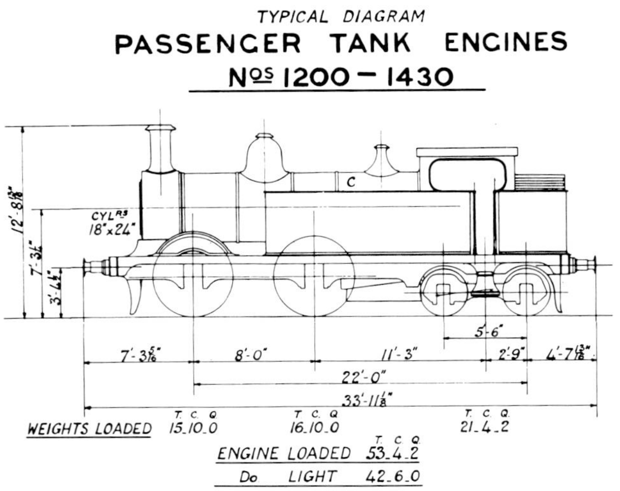

ENGINE Nos	BLR PRES.	DRG WHEELS	TRACTIVE POWER
1200-1225	140Lbs □"	5'-3" DIA.	13824 Lbs = 6·17 Tons
1226-1235	Do.	5'-4" "	13608 " = 6·07 "
1236-1265	Do.	5'-7" "	12998 " = 5·80 "
1266-1350	Do.	5'-4" "	13608 " = 6·07 "
1351-1430	150Lbs □"	" "	14580 " = 6·50 "

ED 1/82

Fig. 7. ED 1/82 is a perfect example of the dangers of using 'typical' diagrams and has been included partly to make this point. It is actually a drawing of the '2228' class but additionally records the boiler pressure and official tractive power for all the various 0–4–4s in service at the time it was issued. *Authors' Collection*

Plate 46. The five Dübs-built '2228' class 0–4–4Ts ran as condenser-fitted engines but there was some renewal and refitting with this batch. Here No. 2229 displays the full crimson lake livery style used on this class during the early years of the century. Note the lamp irons and combined destination brackets. This locomotive was to become No. 1382 in 1907 and British Railways No. 58073 following Nationalisation. Withdrawal took place in 1956. *Collection Roger Carpenter*

Plates 47 & 48. The ten Derby-built 0–4–4T engines of 1898 differed slightly in having straight 'levers' to the Salter safety valves. Most of the '2228' class had curved 'levers', at least when built. These views show No. 783 (later No. 1410) and No. 1403 (originally No. 692), both showing this feature and fairly immaculately turned out in full Johnson livery and early LMS red livery respectively. Livery apart, the main differences between these two views are in the 'front end' configuration. No. 783 is recorded as having been photographed at Melton Mowbray in April 1907. If so, it is surprising that some changes in either livery, numbering or 'anatomy' had not begun to appear.

Authors' Collection

Plate 49. No. 2625 (later No. 1425) and No. 2626 (*Plate 50*) both emerged from Dübs in 1900, yet by the time this and the next view were taken, some slight decorative differences had appeared. Note, for example, the lining on the angle crank at the rear of the brake linkage — not present on No. 2626 — yet No. 2625 has simpler lining on the wheel bosses. This view is undated — probably c.1903.
Authors' Collection

Plate 50. No. 2626 was to become No. 1426 in 1907 and No. 58089 before being withdrawn in 1954. Seen here at St. Albans in July 1902, this locomotive displays the full crimson lake livery as built which included lining out the cab front around the spectacle plates and extra lines on the wheel bosses. Compare also with No. 2229 (*Plate 46*). That locomotive has lining on the small splashers (which are necessary to allow the cranks to revolve), whereas on No. 2626 they are plain crimson lake.
Collection Ken Nunn

Plate 51. No. 1381 entered service in 1895 as No. 2228 and was withdrawn by the LMS at the end of 1933. At the time it was photographed (Kentish Town, May 1922), it retained its continuous handrail but had been fitted with a dished smokebox door. Note the lamp irons and destination board brackets.
Collection A. G. Ellis

Plate 52. As No. 2630, No. 1430 was the last 0-4-4T to be built for the Midland Railway and is seen here at Bourne in 1912 in simplified crimson lake livery. It was a fairly late withdrawal in 1956 as BR No. 58091. The reader's attention is also drawn to the 'solid' coal rails to the side but 'open' coal rails to the rear of the bunker (see also *Plate 53.*
Collection V. R. Anderson

Plate 53. We have included this view of No. 1409 (originally No. 782) to complement *Plate 52* by giving an opposite side *rear* view of this characteristic type. Note, this time, the 'open' coal rails. The engine is, of course, in simplified Deeley livery and was probably photographed at about the same time as *Plate 52*. Note the 'continuous' front hand rail. *Authors' Collection*

Plates 54 & 55. These two pictures illustrate 'old' No. 2616 following renumbering in 1907. *Plate 54* shows No. 1416 in Midland Railway ownership in simplified crimson lake livery. Note the Dübs works plate on the bunker side. *Plate 55* illustrates No. 1416 in LMS pre-1928 crimson lake livery which is almost identical to that of the Midland era. However, since, by the date of this photograph, a Belpaire boiler had been fitted, this has produced a new cab with altered side sheets and lining arrangement. These views clearly show, on both locomotives, the new simplified lining with only the leading boiler lagging band lined and, apart from the wheel tyres, no lining below the platform at all. Finally, note that under LMS ownership the Dübs works plate has been replaced by an 'LMS Rebuilt 1925 Derby' plate on the bunker side and a transferred power class '1' has been applied. *Collections Bernard Mathews and Roger Carpenter*

Plates 56 & 57. Whilst only two footplate views have been used to represent these locomotives, it should be noted that from the pictures in the authors' collection, several more subtle variations could have been illustrated but for space considerations. *Plate 56* taken c.1912 shows No. 1284 and it should be noted that only one steam valve for an injector is visible on the left-hand side of the cab, whereas *Plate 57*, also taken c.1912, shows engine No. 1252. Discussions with elderly Midland Railway drivers have failed to confirm the use for all the controls shown in a number of these footplate views, so contributions from readers would be welcome.

National Railway Museum

Plate 58. This works grey livery picture of No. 2000 clearly illustrates the painting style and condition of this class when built. Note the lining details with none along the valance or on the footsteps. No. 2000 was superheated in 1926 and withdrawn in 1937. Note, too, the heraldic emblem. The Deeley 0–6–4Ts were the only Midland-designed tank engines to carry such a feature, although there is a picture of an 0–4–0ST with the diamond shape device. This, we feel, must have been applied in error. *British Railways*

CHAPTER TWO

THE DEELEY 0-6-4 TANKS

Plate 59. No. 2008 just prior to the grouping. Superheated in 1925, this locomotive was withdrawn in 1936. *Authors' Collection*

THIS series of forty locomotives were all built at Derby in 1907 and were numbered 2000-39 under the new system. In consequence, they were never renumbered, the last member of the class being scrapped in 1938. The first twenty were built to order No. 3187 and the second batch to order 3258. In their original condition they were, in 1910, allocated to Engine Diagram 114 and, following rebuilding with superheated G7S Belpaire boiler, they were allocated to engine diagram 114A. All of them reached the LMS in 1923.

They were first employed mainly upon the suburban services around Manchester and Birmingham which required a more powerful locomotive than the existing 0–6–0Ts, 0–4–4Ts and 2–4–0s. Water pick-up apparatus was provided, as far as we know, on only one member of the class, No. 2015, and from 1920 onwards the engines were fitted with superheated boilers with Belpaire fireboxes, the first one thus dealt with being No. 2035. The smokebox was extended to accommodate the superheater header, but otherwise there was little alteration in appearance, save for the firebox itself, of course, and alterations to cab front spectacle plate.

Some locomotives spent much of their life at certain sheds and during 1939 the *SLS Journal* dealt with a number of aspects of the class including some details of their work on the LT & S section, which we now reproduce with due acknowledgements.

'In 1913-4, six of the class were fitted with Westinghouse brake and transferred to Tilbury section. The intention was for them to replace the standard 4–4–2T on the heaviest trains; but, although test runs were made, the results of these showed that the 0–6–4Ts were not speedy enough to keep booked time. Although they were for a short time used (bunker first) to work such trains as the 6.26 p.m. from Fenchurch St. to Barking (where one of the 'Baltics' took charge) they were unable to stand up to the thrashing they received and were soon relegated to shunting and goods work.

'During their period on Tilbury line passenger work they suffered such casualties as bent piston rods, sheared off coupling rod crank-pins, and a wheel shifting on its axle due to a hot driving axle box. Bunker first they rode very comfortably, and indeed could not always be called rough riders even engine first; although they had a definite 'nosing' action due to the combination of side play in the leading Cartazzi coupled axle boxes and the mass of the long forward extension of the side tanks. It was these, in conjunction with the inspection opening in the tanks which caused the engines to be known variously as 'Flatirons' or 'Pom poms' or 'Hole in the Wall tanks'. All had been returned to the Midland line by 1915, whereupon they resumed their normal suburban work.

'After a quarter of a century of fairly hard work, these engines came under a cloud, owing to a number of derailments when employed on passenger turns. One of these resulted in the death of a driver. They were subsequently relegated to slow goods and shunting jobs to wear themselves out working to a 45 mph speed limit.'

Over the years much has been written about this class and we believe that it would not be inappropriate to place the facts which came to light in the MOT Accident Report on record and below is an extract from this document.

'To deal with goods traffic, the engine was provided with larger water and coal capacity than is usual for a tank engine of this size and type, viz., 2,250 gallons, or 10 tons, of water, and 3½ tons of coal. The side tanks are extended nearly to the front of the smoke box, and having regard to the distribution of weight

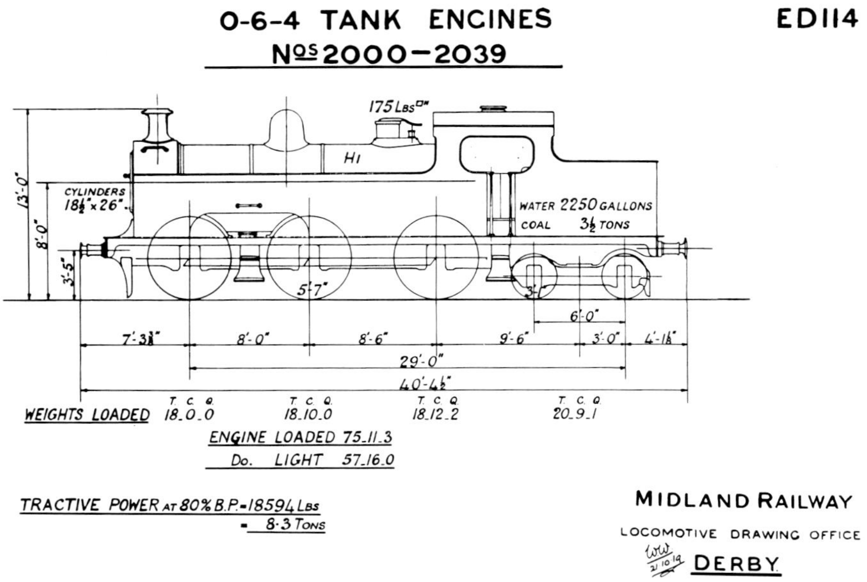

Fig. 8. Engine Diagram 114. This is the 1919 Midland Railway diagram for this class when in saturated condition.
National Railway Museum

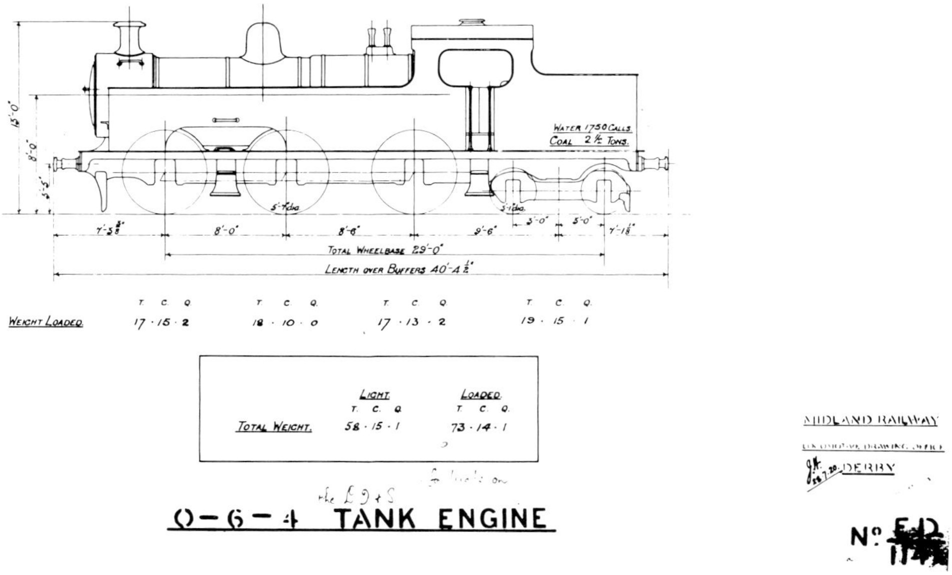

Fig. 9. Engine Diagram 114A is a copy of a diagram dated 26th July 1920 which shows the class in superheated condition. However, the diagram is specially interesting insofar as it refers to locomotives which were to be sent to the LT & S section and suggests that the water capacity was to be reduced to 1,750 gallons from the 2,250 in their normal condition and that coal capacity was to be reduced from 3½ to 2½ tons.
National Railway Museum

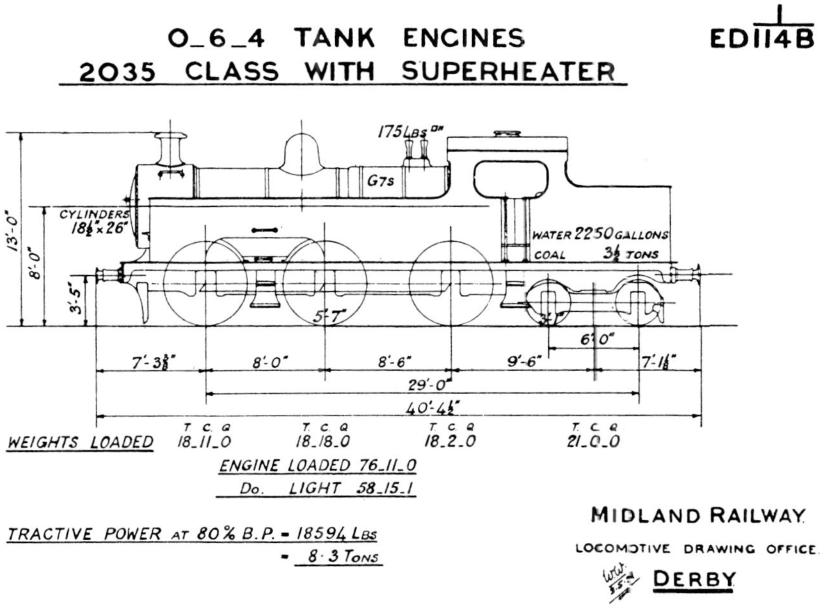

Fig. 10. This further diagram ED 1/114B is dimensionally identical to ED 114A except that it confirms a water capacity of 2,250 gallons and 3½ tons of coal for 'No. 2035 class with superheater' – No. 2035 being the first member of the class to be rebuilt. *Authors' Collection*

of water and coal there is clearly a high moment of inertia about the vertical axis.

'The engine was designed to negotiate curves of 6 chs. radius; flexibility in the wheel base was attained in two ways, by side play (¼ inch total) of the six coupled axle boxes in their guides, and by the incorporation of Cartazzi slides in the leading axle boxes, play on the latter account being 1 inch from one side to the other, controlled by lubricated slides of 1 in 8 inclination. These slides were in good condition, and depending on friction and the state of compression of the coil bearing springs, they exerted a minimum lateral controlling force of roughly 2 tons 6 cwts. The white metal pads on the outside faces of these axle boxes were slightly marked by the bosses of the wheel centres, showing that the side play provided had been utilised to the full extent in service.

'With regard to the bogie design, in addition to the side movement as a whole of 2 ⅞ inches each way, total play of ¼ inch was allowed for each axle in respect of the axle boxes in their guides. This had become increased by wear in engine No. 2023, as already noted; the bearing surfaces, being comparatively small, permitted the development of early sloppiness. The controlling force of the bogie check springs rises from ⅝ ton to 2¾ tons, so that the rear end of the engine, with its heavy load of coal and water, is comparatively lightly controlled in the first stages of side-to-side displacement.

'As might be expected, the engine can easily negotiate sharp curvature at low speed, but this advantage has to be paid for by unsteadiness at high speed, and, as pointed out in previous reports upon other tank engine derailments, it is very sensitive to defective track conditons, in that comparatively small variations of gauge or line may initiate oscillation which, as I noted on the footplate, was accentuated under steam.

'Undamped by a heavy separate tender, the engine has, in fact, a natural frequency of oscillation depending on such factors as weight distribution, the periodicity of the front coil springs, the Cartazzi slides, the laminated bogie check springs, and the action of steam in the cylinders. Should track variations, insufficient in themselves to cause serious movement in a less sensitive machine, follow in sequence so as to coincide sufficiently closely with the engine's natural frequency under the conditions of the moment, oscillation may be rapidly and violently induced, and therefore heavy lateral forces may be set up, which in turn tend to displace the track bodily, or, if fastenings are sufficiently weak, to spread the gauge.

Remarks and Recommendations.

'17.– (a) Having regard to the foregoing considerations and to the circumstances of this derailment, it was decided to make a trial under the following altered conditions, viz. the replacement of the leading axle Cartazzi boxes and of the coil springs by standard type boxes and laminated springs; the replacement of the bogie by a standard bogie with side bolsters, as used on the new 2–6–4 type tank engines; and the replacement of the screw reversing gear by a lever gear to facilitate the use of the engine for shunting purposes.

'As a result, comparative tests, at speeds varying from 35 to 60 m.p.h., with one engine so modified and another not altered, were carried out a few days after the derailment at Moira, on a straight length of 2nd class track. The conclusion was reached that the unmodified engines were not suitable for working trains at speeds over 45 m.p.h., and, indeed, I was informed that severe oscillation was experienced at no more than 50 m.p.h., the passage of the engine causing some track damage. On the other hand, I understand that the alterations undoubtedly made for improvement, oscillation and roll being damped out, so that even when running at 60 m.p.h., the riding was satisfactory.

'Having regard, however, to the facts that these engines now possess superheated boilers of standard design, which can be

Plates 60 & 61 (opposite). These views give opposite sides of Nos. 2000/1 in Midland Railway livery when in saturated condition. The question of the cab roof colour is not easy to resolve. One old driver claims that they were red all over, whereas we believe that some were probably black between the rain strips. The lining ended at the rainstrip, that is certain, but one cannot be sure of the colour of the top of the cab roof and ventilator. No. 2001 was superheated in 1925 and withdrawn in 1937. *Roger Carpenter Collection and Peter Truman*

Plate 62. Some 0–6–4Ts went to the LT & SR section for trials and were equipped with Westinghouse brakes. These were Nos. 2004/11/13/24/34/35 and at least one of them, No. 2035, retained the Westinghouse brake gear until they were superheated. However, No. 2035, photographed at Derby on 24th July 1920, illustrates this brake gear on a superheated engine and we are unable to say when it was removed from all of these locomotives. No. 2035 was superheated in 1920 and was withdrawn in 1936. *W. L. Good*

Plate 63. Saturated 0–6–4T No. 2004 at Plaistow when Westinghouse fitted for work on the LT & S Section. *K. Leech*

utilised for other engines, and that modern tank engines with lighter axle loading and higher tractive effort were becoming available, the Company decided that the above-mentioned alterations were not justified, and the majority of the engines have been taken out of service with a view to early scrapping and the release of the boilers for use elsewhere; a certain number have been left in goods traffic for the time being, subject to a maximum speed of 45 m.p.h.

'(b) A speed restriction of 40 m.p.h. has also been imposed on the branch line between Evesham and Ashchurch. This is a necessary protective precaution for the time being, pending the renewal proposed for 1936, as already mentioned, of some 2 miles of the down line covering the site of the accident, on the falling gradient between Hinton and Ashton-under-Hill where high speed is possible; in addition, the relaying of 2 miles of the same line, between Ashton-under-Hill and Beckford has already been approved for 1935. Similar proposals are in hand for the up line.

'While I was informed that essential repairs will be effected forthwith, and I am aware of the extent of the efforts which have been made in the last few years to deal with renewals in this Division, I feel that the policy of 'spot' replacement of sleepers should, if practicable, be discontinued, and that the renewal programme on this branch should be accelerated. The circumstances of this accident appear to show that unless conditions are abnormal, such as unusually rapid decay of timber, the merits of this method of maintenance are very questionable.

'(c) With regard to the classification of this branch, it seems doubtful whether it did in fact bear a true relation to the speed and character of the traffic. Apart from the evidence of the District Engineer and of the Chief Permanent Way Inspector, there is the significant factor that, under the Company's progressive policy of scrapping older types of engine, the building of new, heavier, and speedier units is making rapid strides. I suggest that the whole question of the classification of branch lines, not only in respect of bridge loading, but of track fitness for speed in relation to types of engines, requires review, and that at the same time closer liaison between the Departments concerned should be maintained, so that speed maxima may be regulated in accordance with the authority of the responsible Engineer.

'This matter also seems to warrant consideration from the economic aspect; the operation of this particular type of tank engine has, for example, probably caused much avoidable expenditure, as the result of abnormal track damage during recent years, following the efforts to increase speed. Apart from its tendency to destructive oscillation, the total hammer-blow of the engine amounts to 2.29 tons at 60 m.p.h., while those of individual axles are substantially higher, amounting to 9.66 tons in the case of the driving axle.

'(d) In this connection generally, the value of the information to be gained from riding on the footplate by those responsible for maintenance of permanent way is of importance, and is recognised by the instructions issued on the subject. There could have been no better practical instrument than this type of engine for ascertaining where track defects exist, and I think that the instructions might well be more definite that Permanent Way Inspectors should make a regular practice of thus travelling over branch lines, as well as over main lines.

I have the honour to be,
Sir,
Your obedient Servant,
A. H. L. MOUNT, *Lieut.-Colonel.*

The Secretary,
Ministry of Transport.'

As we went to press, some LMS internal correspondence came to light and this is reproduced exactly as it was written:

Chief Mechanical Engineer's Office
EUSTON

M.
G.21DC/14/6 1st April 1935

2000 Class Tank Engine, Trial Runs between Weston-on-Trent and Lock Lane Crossing, Sunday, 31st March 1935

ENGINE TESTED No. 2000 which had been modified as follows:-

Improved bogie with side bolsters, leading Cartazzi boxes with coil springs replaced by standard type of box and laminated springs and also screw reversing gear removed and a lever gear fitted.

This engine is just out of Derby Shops after General Repairs.

Engine No. 2012

This engine is of the standard type and had a General Repair on 13th February 1935 and has not yet completed 1000 miles. Both the foregoing engines are therefore in first-class running condition.

OBJECT OF THE TEST

To ascertain by actual running tests the comparative riding performance of these two engines when running at speeds of 35, 45 and 55 m.p.h., these particulars to be noted on lengths of straight road where side oscillation develops with this type of engine.

Observations were made by C.M.E. representatives on the footplate and Engineer's staff noted the running of the engine and the effect on the permanent way.

A 6-wheeled passenger brake was attached to the engine (the engine worked all the tests on the up line running chimney first) and this van was fitted up with a 'Flaman' speed recorder giving a true indication of the actual speeds at which the tests were run. A Cambridge accelerometer was fitted on the leading buffer beam of each engine, which recorded oscillation and vertical movement of the engine at this position.

On Engine 2000 a special instrument was fitten which recorded the relative side movement of the trailing 4-wheeled bogie relative to the engine main frames, but it was not possible to fit up this instrument on Engine 2012.

LOCALITY

The trials were carried out on the Castle Donington Branch, the actual running tests being carried out between Viaduct No. 14, which had a speed restriction of 20 m.p.h., and Viaduct No. 6, which had a speed restriction of 15 m.p.h. The length of track available was 3¼ miles, and from information supplied this is a Class 2 road with 60 ft. lengths of rail.

There is a speed restriction on this portion of road of 45 m.p.h. for 2000 class engines, but it was agreed that if the riding of the engines were considered satisfactory, higher speeds could be run at the discretion of the C.M.E. representative.

The particulars obtained from observation on the engine footplate are as follows:-

ENGINE NO. 2000 fitted with Modified Bogie etc.

Test No. 1 35 m.p.h. For the first ½ mile, the engine ran between 35 and 50 m.p.h. and then settled down to 35.	**The engine rode very steadily.** No side movement was recorded of trailing bogie.
Test No. 2 45 m.p.h. The speed varied between 45 and 50 m.p.h. for the first portion of the run, then settled down to 45.	**Steady riding.** No movement of bogie indicated.

Plates 64 & 65. These two pictures illustrate No. 2038 in Midland and LMS ownership. No. 2038 was superheated in 1926 and was therefore returned to service still painted in LMS crimson lake (*Plate 64*). While it is not possible to date this photograph, it was after the introduction of the P & F suffix in 1928 as can be seen from the upper cabside markings. *Plate 65* is an earlier view of No. 2038 in Midland livery, in saturated condition and with a dished Deeley smokebox door – compare with *Plate 58*. The photograph was taken at Bourneville on 31st August 1919.

Photomatic and W. L. Good

Plate 66. This near frontal view of superheated No. 2022 in early LMS days makes an interesting detail comparison with *Plate 65.* The engine was superheated in 1925 and scrapped ten years later. *Authors' Collection*

Test No. 3 55 m.p.h.

Speed varied slightly and occasionally touched 60 m.p.h.	Good riding. No movement of bogie indicated.

The good riding qualities of Engine 2000 with the modified bogie were such that it was considered quite safe to try out a speed of 60-65 m.p.h. as follows:-

Test No. 4 60 m.p.h.

The speed varied between 60 and 67 m.p.h. but settled down to about 65. A slight amount of side oscillation developed and a slight roll, but could be considered	satisfactory riding.

ENGINE NO. 2012 This engine was tried out under the standard conditions of this class of engine.

Test No. 1 35 m.p.h.

The engine occasionally touched 40 m.p.h. but settled down to 35.	The riding was good but a slight oscillation and a slight roll were perceptible on the footplate.

Test No. 2 45 m.p.h.

Occasionally this speed was exceeded, the maximum being 47.	Riding fairly good but more oscillation noted and a tendency to roll.

Test No. 3 55 m.p.h.

The speed occasionally on this trip touched 60 m.p.h., but settled down to 55.	Riding was rough, the oscillation and roll pronounced and there was a tendency for the front end to develop an up-and-down surging movement. This was particularly noted at 60 m.p.h.

From the foregoing particulars, it would appear that these 0–6–4 tank engines may be considered suitable for working trains up to about 50 m.p.h. provided the permanent way is in good condition and it will also be noted that the engine is in very good condition, having only run a bare 1000 miles.

These engines, when fitted with the modified 4-wheeled trailing bogie and the modifications to the leading coupled wheel, proved to be undoubtedly much better riding engines, the tendency to oscillation and roll being damped out and even running at speeds of 60 m.p.h. the riding was quite satisfactory.

See Cambridge accelerometer records attached.

TEST TO BE CARRIED OUT WITH THE 2000 TYPE OF ENGINE BETWEEN KIBWORTH AND GREAT GLEN

Mr. Darby will inform me the date on which this test is to take place, this test being between 88¾ to 91¼ miles, Down Road, the actual speed test taking place between 90 and 91¼ miles.

The day before the test is to be carried out the road is to be gauged and canted at each joint and middle of rail and the 6 ft. checked at every 2nd or 3rd joint between 90 and 91¼ miles.

On the day of the test, the road between these mileages must again be gauged and the cant taken as above immediately after the 55 m.p.h. run.

Mr. Horton will supply the necessary platelayers to assist the Technical Staff from this Office in the taking of the necessary cants and gauges.

Messrs. Beastall and Walker will take the gauges and cant both on the day before the run and on the day of the run and it will be necessary for Mr. Horton to have two men present at Great Glen for the measurements to be taken on the day preceding the test run and on the day of the run it will be necessary to have two men at the 90 m.p. and 2 at the 91¼ m.p.

* * *

E. G. Horton, Esq.,
District Engineer,
NORTHAMPTON — 1st April 1935

TEST TO BE CARRIED OUT WITH THE 2000 TYPE OF ENGINE BETWEEN KIBWORTH AND GREAT GLEN

With reference to conversation.

I shall be much obliged if you will arrange for two men to be at Great Glen Station at 10.46 a.m. on the day before the actual test runs are to be made.

Plate 67. This high level view of superheated No. 2037 leaving Cofton Tunnel in June 1926 shows clear 'tank top' detail of the Deeley 0–6–4T design.
W. L. Good

On the day of the test runs I shall be glad if you will arrange for two men to be present at the 90 M.P. and two men at the 91¼ M.P.

These men to be in position a quarter of an hour before the time of the first run.

Signed. H. B. EVERARD

From District Engineer's Office,
Castle Station,
NORTHAMPTON

H. B. Everard, Esq.,
Derby S.

TEST TO BE CARRIED OUT WITH THE 2000 TYPE
OF ENGINE BETWEEN KIBWORTH AND GREAT GLEN.

I am in receipt of your letter of the 1st instant in regard to the above, and am arranging in accordance therewith.

Signed E. G. HORTON

From Divisional Engineer's Office
DERBY

H. B. Everard, Esq.

April 3rd 1935

TESTS WITH 2000 TYPE PASSENGER TANK ENGINES

With reference to your letter of the 1st April.

I am now informed that as a result of the test Mr. Stanier considers that it would not be worth while taking any further tests with these engines and that they are not worth altering.

This is for your information.

Signed E. G. HORTON

From Divisional Engineer's Office
DERBY

H. B. Everard, Esq.

April 5th 1935

TESTS WITH 2000 TYPE PASSENGER TANK ENGINES

With reference to your letter of the 1st instant.

I send you herewith for your information and return a copy of a report Mr. Wallace has received from Mr. Stanier hereon.

E. G. Horton, Esq.,
NORTHAMPTON

5th April 1935

TESTS WITH 2000 TYPE PASSENGER TANK ENGINES

With reference to my letter of 1st instant and yours of 2nd.

I have now heard from Mr. Darby that as a result of the test which took place last Sunday, Mr. Stanier considers it would not be worth while taking any further tests with these engines and that they would not be worth altering.

In consequence the arrangement set forth in my letter of 1st instant may now be cancelled.

Signed H. B. EVERARD

The 0–6–4T was an unusual wheel configuration and, though not unique to the Midland, was never widely regarded in Britain. Indeed, one has to search hard to find praiseworthy comments about any of the various examples of the type built in this country, so maybe one should not castigate the MR examples in isolation; they were not alone in their inadequacies. What is, however, interesting is that at the very time that Deeley introduced them, the Derby drawing office had schemed out several alternative forms of large suburban tank, all of rather better intrinsic soundness than the 0–6–4Ts and any one of which would have been a far better basis for development. A further discussion of this interesting aspect of the Midland's policy will be found in Chapter 6. Meantime, back to the engines which were built.

Compared with many Midland designs, this class did not survive long enough to undergo any really dramatic changes in appearance, by far the most obvious being those occasioned by the aforementioned fitting of superheated Belpaire boilers from 1920 and afterwards. During MR days, this had only affected a trio (Nos. 2002/35/9), but the LMS rapidly completed the task, the whole class being converted by 1927.

Midland livery was equally consistent. They came out in the simplified Deeley crimson lake with large 18 in. tank side numberals and, uniquely for MR-designed tank locomotives, were given the new 1907 MR heraldic emblem on the bunker side. This distinction they shared with no other tank types save those inherited from the LT & SR, but these, of course, were not 'pure' MR designs. After 1923, red was retained until 1928 with LMS markings, after which the LMS lined black livery became universal. Their final years are considered in more detail in our LMS survey and we conclude this section with a further selection of detailed views of this distinctive if not totally successful type.

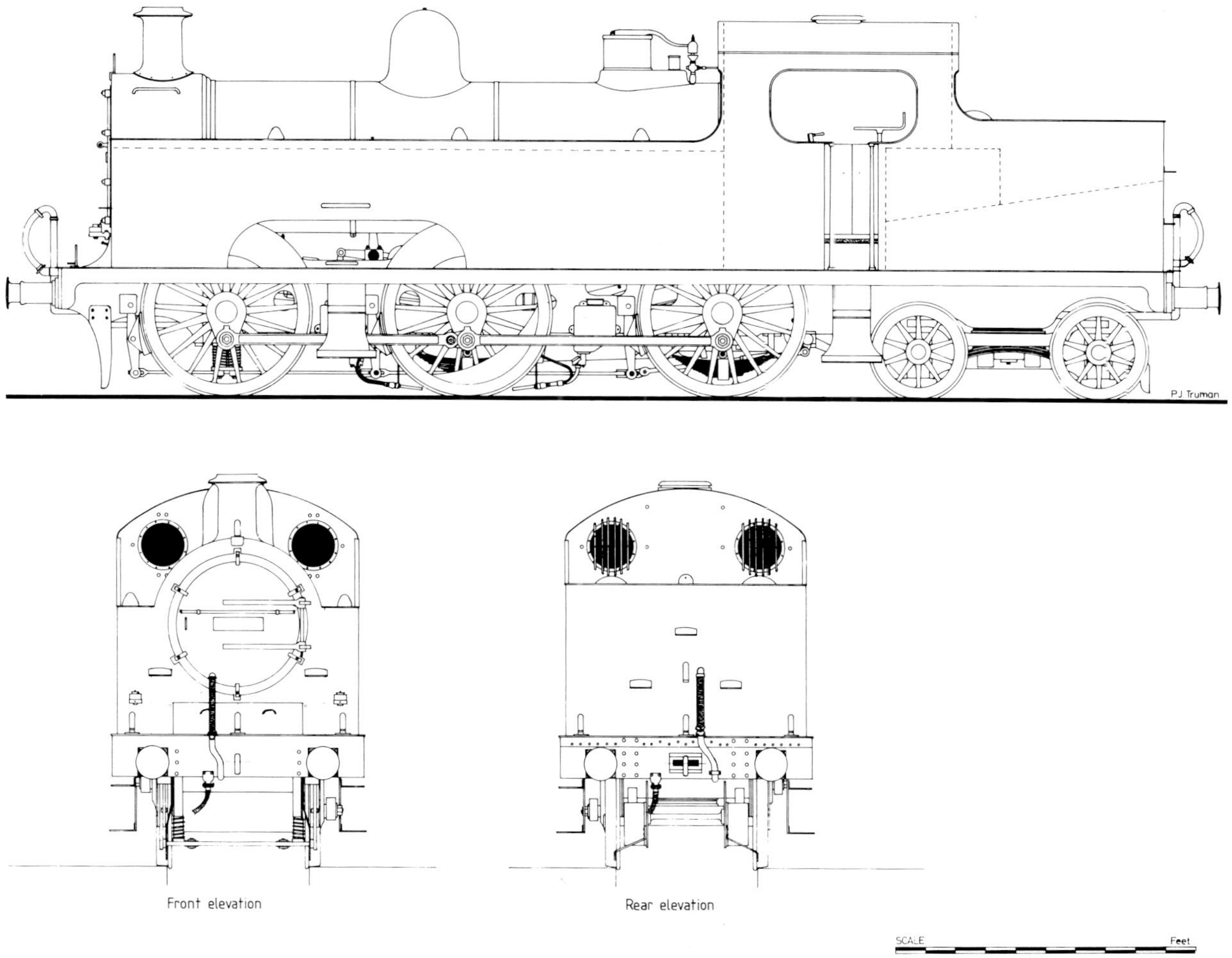

Fig. 11. For all their poor press, the 'Flat-irons' have always been popular with modellers. The excellent draughtsmanship is by Peter Truman and shows the saturated form. *Peter Truman*

Plate 68. Superheated No. 2018 is seen here ex works in LMS lined black livery and was photographed on 26th March 1929. Note the Ramsbottom safety valves, later to be replaced with Ross Pops. Note also that bogie brakes have again been fitted (see also *Plate 69*). Pictures taken in the Midland period do not show this equipment. No. 2018 was withdrawn in 1937.

British Railways

Plate 69. No. 2005 in LMS lined black livery. This locomotive is also equipped with bogie brakes – a not uncommon late MR/early LMS feature. We are unable to say how many members of this class were so equipped but we have recorded Nos. 2005/12/16-21/29. No. 2005 was withdrawn in 1936 having been superheated ten years earlier. *Authors' Collection*

Plate 70. This opposite side view of superheated No. 2002, also in LMS lined black livery, was taken at Toton in 1936, towards the end of its life. No. 2002 was superheated in 1921 and withdrawn in 1937. *Authors' Collection*

Plate 71. Two locomotives from this series were withdrawn before the 1907 renumbering, Nos. 1429A and No. 202. This picture shows No. 1429A probably a year or so before withdrawal (1905) in lined crimson lake livery and still with its original wheels. *Authors' Collection*

Plate 72. No. 1323A in crimson lake livery, now equipped with a cab and running with replacement wheels. Compare with No. 1322 as built (*Plate 73*). Becoming No. 1501 in 1907, this locomotive was withdrawn in 1921. *Authors' Collection*

CHAPTER THREE

YARD SHUNTING ENGINES

ALTHOUGH the Midland's goods traffic was normally handled by 0–6–0 locomotives, tender or tank, both on the main line and in yards, there was, nevertheless, a number of four-coupled tank locomotives, and all but a handful of these are described within this chapter. Those which are not featured were a few locomotives mostly taken over from the Staveley Coal and Iron Company, all of which were withdrawn by the turn of the century. The story of these locomotives will be given in Volume 6.

The 0–4–0Ts built by the Midland fell into two main groups, designed by Johnson and Deeley respectively. The thirty Johnson engines were of the saddle tank configuration, whilst Deeley was responsible for ten side tanks. The Johnson saddle tanks were officially divided into three quite separate sub-groups (see Table 2) but all three of these sub-divisions shared very similar lines. They were quite unlike any other Johnson engines but, equally, their appearance had little in common with any other contemporary design of 0–4–0ST. They were built in batches of five over quite a long period of time, and towards the end of their days they tended to be regarded as one single class. In this respect, they followed the pattern of many Midland engines, and this latter-day tendency to lump different diagrams into one single class helps explain why the history of Midland engines is often hard to understand.

The Deeley engines were also built in two batches, the second coming into service during the Fowler period. In the survey which follows, we deal with each of the groups according to their original classification.

We begin our review with a series of ten locomotives all built at Derby in two batches. The first engine at least, and possibly the first batch, were constructed with just a weather-board (see *Plate 73*) but pictorial evidence indicates that this was replaced by a new cab roof, which was turned backwards with a rear upward flare, and that later engines were built like this. This was supported by two round pillars attached to a rear, half-height, cab panel – it must have been a very cold footplate in winter! Finally an 'all over cab' appeared on some locomotives and to date we have confirmed that Nos. 1504, 1506 (1907 numbers), later to be renumbered 1509 and 1507, were so equipped, but there may have been others.

They were employed upon shunting duties in areas where they were more suitable than six-coupled engines, for example certain docks, breweries and collieries, where the sharp curve radii prevented the use of a six-coupled engine.

In their original condition they were, eventually, all painted in lined Crimson Lake, but the first five, built in 1883, came into service just in time to receive a green livery for a few years. However, we feel certain that they were

Plate 73. No. 1322 in works grey. Becoming No. 1500 in 1907, this locomotive was to be withdrawn in 1926. Note the straight weatherboard and open back at the rear of the locomotive. We believe that the first five were built in this condition but, as noted in the text, they were altered with two different styles of cab roof being employed.
Authors' Collection

probably all red *before* cab roofs replaced weatherboards (above). The view of No. 1322 at *Plate 73* shows the 'as built' configuration and, since it is of the pioneer example in works grey livery, it seems reasonable to assume that the view represents the short-lived 'green' period for the first five engines.

They ran in Crimson Lake until c.1910, by which time plain black became the order of the day. Interestingly, the 1907 renumbering saw some of these locomotives with brass numerals and it was probably not until c.1910, when they began to go into black livery, that transferred numerals began to be employed. It is recorded that one engine (No. 1517) ran with the early heraldic device, the only record of a tank locomotive other than the 0–6–4T to be so treated.

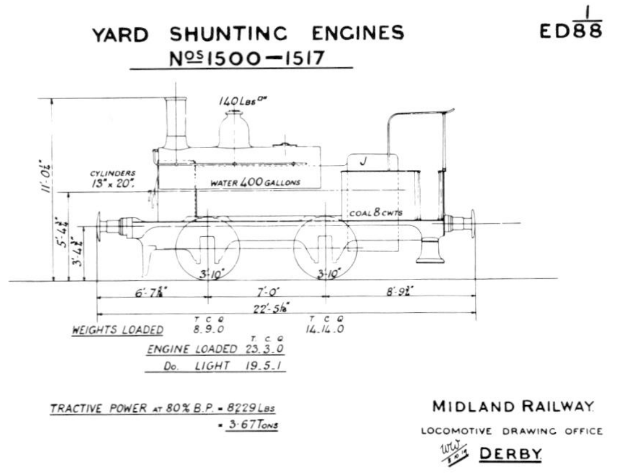

Fig. 12. This 1919 diagram refers to the series of locomotives which in 1907 had become Nos. 1500-1517.
National Railway Museum

Apart from acquiring cab roofs, the most obvious other difference after their original construction was the wheels. As built they had square or 'H' section spokes whereas later more conventional spokes are to be seen (see various plates).

We have not been able to trace an earlier Engine Diagram than ED 88 which was issued in October 1919 and was used to cover the old '1322' and '1116' series. This has been reproduced at *Fig. 12.*

1322 CLASS

Summary

Ten locomotives were built at Derby, five in 1883 and five in 1889/90.

Their original Midland Railway numbers were 1322-1326, 202, 1428-1430, 1697. In 1892 the entire class was placed upon the duplicate list as 1322A etc. and in 1907 they were renumbered 1500-1507 (Nos. 202A and 1429A were withdrawn before being renumbered). No. 1506 was renumbered 1509 in 1930 by the LMS.

They were all allocated to Engine Diagram 88 in 1919 by the Midland Railway.

Plate 74. By now No. 1324 has been renumbered 1502 and when compared with No. 1322 it has acquired 'a cab' with a solid rear panel to the footplate. This feature can also be seen in the earlier views of 1323A and 1429A. When photographed, the locomotive was in plain black livery. Note the retention of the original wheels. Withdrawal was in 1924. *Authors' Collection*

Plates 75 & 76. These two pictures have been chosen to illustrate the last survivor of the class, old No. 1430 which became No. 1506 in 1907 and was renumbered 1509 in 1930. By 1928 the remainder of the class had been withdrawn but this locomotive lasted until the end of 1949. The views were taken at Derby Works in 1931 and 1945 respectively. *G. Coltas and Authors' Collection*

1116A CLASS

A second series of 0–4–0STs was built at Derby in the 1890s and eight out of the ten constructed went straight onto the duplicate list with 'A' numbers. It should be noted that whilst they were originally built with open back cabs, photographic evidence confirms that at least Nos. 1510 and 1511 received closed cabs as illustrated (see *Plate 79*).

An interesting point concerned the placing of the numbers with the 1116A and 1322 class. Those which were originally capital list and then duplicated had the four figures central, with the 'A' offset to the right, which meant that the whole new duplicated number was 'off centre'; those which were built new for the duplicate list had all five characters of the entire number, i.e. including the letter 'A', placed centrally on the panel.

This second series of 0–4–0STs, apart from some quite trivial changes in boiler tubing and fractional weight variation (see *Table 2*), were, to all intents and purposes, a repeat of the '1322' class and most railways would have regarded all twenty engines as being of the same type. They certainly displayed no significant differences in appearance. In fact, there was more visual difference between an 'open' and 'closed' cab locomotive within either one of the two groups than there was between engines of the two groups themselves.

Plate 77. This view of No. 1120A illustrates the painting style when first built and shows that this batch had an open 'cab', hence the increase in weight (see *Table 2*). No. 1120A was later to become No. 1512 and ran as such until withdrawal in 1921. Note the original wheels in this view and also *Plate 79* (No. 1511).

Authors' Collection

Summary

Ten locomotives were built at Derby, five in 1893 and five in 1897. Their original Midland Railway numbers were 1116A-1120A, 2359-2360, 1131A-1133A and in 1907 the Midland Railway re-numbered them 1508-1517. The class was extinct by 1955. No separate Engine Diagram has been found; they were allocated to Engine Diagram 88.

Plate 78. No. 1514 was originally No. 2360 built in 1897 and lasted until withdrawal in 1930. It is seen here in plain black Midland Railway livery.

J. H. Wright

Plate 79. This view of No. 1511 shows a locomotive in plain black livery and, being devoid of ownership markings, is thought to date from c.1923 when the engine was probably repainted by the infant LMS before the company ownership markings had been agreed.

Authors' Collection

Plate 80. This picture illustrates No. 1515 in LMS pre-1928 black livery. Originally No. 1131A, this locomotive was withdrawn in 1926.

Authors' Collection

1134A CLASS

A further series of locomotives was built at Derby in two batches and this final series of saddle tanks exhibited a 6 in. longer wheelbase with a longer overhang at both the front and rear, as can be seen from the diagrams and pictures. In all, the series were altogether larger locomotives, but, like their predecessors, they entered service with open back cabs (see Plate 64, page 37, Volume 1).

A considerable increase in boiler size and water capacity was also made in these final 0–4–0STs which, no doubt, helps to explain a large part of the quite substantial weight increase proportional to that of the original 20 engines (see *Table 2*). This gave them a quite noticeably different appearance, though still very much part of the same family. It was best appreciated from a frontal view where the larger diameter boiler, the deeper saddle and the smokebox handrail set well below the top of the saddle, imparted an altogether more powerful look to the engines. This group at least did justify some different form of classification and they were put on a separate Engine Diagram from the first twenty.

Summary

Built at Derby in 1897, Nos. 1134A-1138A, and, in 1903, Nos. 1139A-1143A, all entered service with duplicate numbers. The Midland Railway renumbered them in 1907 and they became Nos. 1518-1527. Two locomotives became British Railways stock and the class was extinct in 1958. They were allocated to ED 1/86 in 1919.

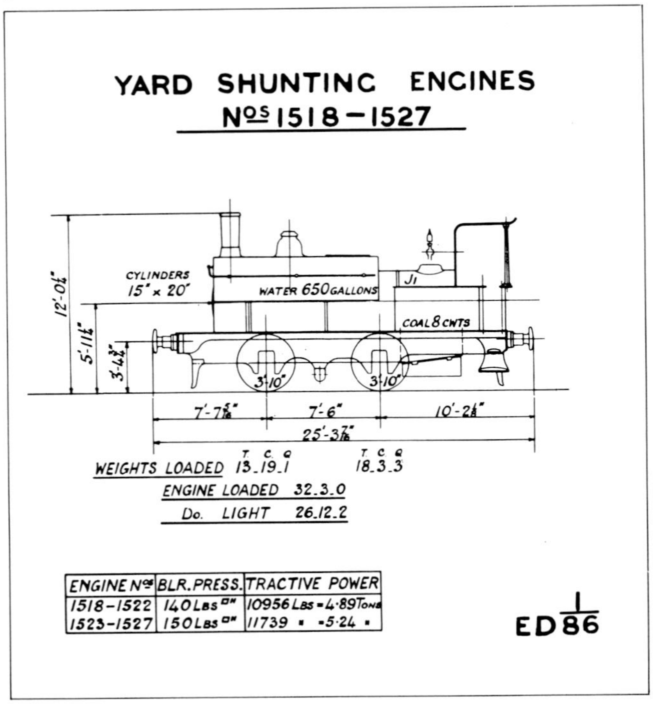

Fig. 13. ED 1/86 was the Midland Railway 1919 diagram for this class and this document confirms the official boiler pressure and tractive power for the class at that date. *Authors' Collection*

Plate 81. No. 1138A in works grey as built in 1897. The locomotive became No. 1522 in 1907 and was withdrawn in 1928.
Authors' Collection

Plate 82. This picture of No. 1523 in Midland Railway ownership depicts old No. 1139A following renumbering in 1907 using brass numerals, but by now it is in plain black livery.
A. G. Ellis

Plate 83. No. 1142A in full crimson lake livery. We illustrated the opposite side of this engine at *Plate 64* in Volume One Built in 1903, this locomotive was to become No. 1527 in 1907 before being withdrawn by the Midland Railway in 1922. *National Railway Museum*

Plate 84. No. 1523 at Gloucester c.1923. Still in Midland Railway black livery, this locomotive was to remain in traffic until 1955 when it was withdrawn as British Railways No. 41523. *W. L. Good*

Plates 85 & 86. No. 1518 in LMS and British railways condition. Built as No. 1134A, it became No. 1518 in 1907 and lasted until 1958. Note the replacement smokebox door which was now closed by six dogs instead of the original central dart. The altogether 'heavier' characteristics of this final group of ten 0–4–0STs is well seen if this view of No. 1518 is compared with that of No. 1515 (*Plate 80*), one of the earlier series photographed from an almost identical angle. *Authors' Collection & British Railways*

1528 CLASS

The final group of four-wheel tank engines to be introduced by the Midland Railway was a class of ten 0—4—0Ts built in two batches, five in 1907 and the remaining five much later, in 1921. They were rather massively proportioned engines and, like the earlier 0—4—0STs, were fitted with stove-pipe chimneys.

Summary

Engine Nos. 1528-32: Built by Midland Railway 1907, Order No. 3031.

Engine Nos. 1533-37: Built by Midland Railway during 1921/2 as renewals for Johnson 0—4—0STs Nos. 1501/12/21/26-7.

Never renumbered, save for addition of 40000 in BR days. Class extinct 1966. Allocated to Midland Railway ED 87.

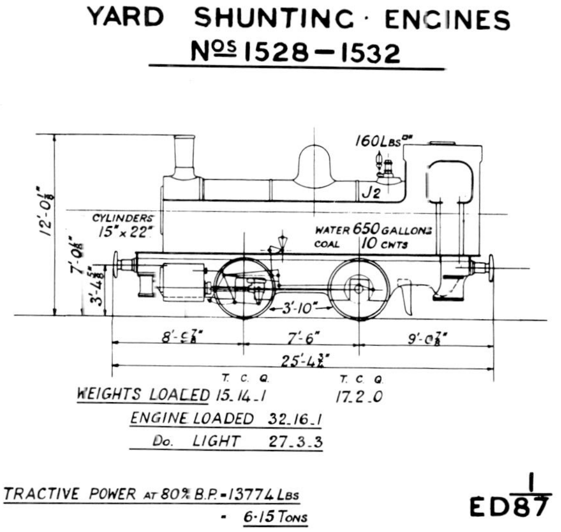

Fig. 14. ED 87 the 1919 MR diagram (suitable amended after 1921), referred to the whole group of ten engines.
Authors' Collection

Plate 87. Engine No. 1528 was given a works grey lined livery when built and as such provides an excellent guide to the simplified Deeley crimson livery applied to the first five engines of the class. As BR No. 41528, this engine, along with No. 41533 of the second series, was one of the last two survivors of the class, both being withdrawn in 1966. *Collection Bernard Mathews*

Plate 88. In this view we see No. 1528 in LMS ownership (see *Plates 92-100* for British Railways era views) of this locomotive. *Authors' Collection*

Plate 89. This picture of No. 1534 of the second series, provides a very clear comparison with the following view of No. 1529. Note the prominent rivet heads and other differences mentioned in the text. As BR No. 41534, this engine was, along with No. 41530, one of the first withdrawals.
Authors' Collection

Plates 90 & 91. These opposite side views of No. 1529 in LMS livery show the running numbers to the left of the 'LMS' on both sides of the engine – a somewhat unusual state of affairs. The theoretically correct version was with the 'LMS' at the chimney end on both sides. As No. 41529, the locomotive survived until 1961. *Authors Collection*

TABLE 2 – JOHNSON & DEELEY 0-4-0T CLASSES

1903 Diagram Page No.	Order No. or Class	Built by	Quantity Built	Date of Building	Pre 1907 Numbers	1907 Renumbering	Cylinders	BOILER					Working Pressure	FIREBOX		Total Heating Surface in Sq Ft	WHEELS		ENGINE WEIGHT		Water Capacity in Gallons	Coal Capacity	REMARKS
								Centre Line	Diameter	Length	Tubes	Diameter		Length	Grate Area in Sq Ft		Driving	Tyres	Empty	Loaded			
81	341	Derby	5	1883	1322-1326	1500-1507	13″ × 20″	5′4½″	3′0″	9′0″	113	1¾″	140 PSI	3′0″	8	534	3′9½″	not quoted	18.18.2	21.14.0	400	8 cwt	1322 class. Entered traffic painted green. Built without cabs.
	816	Derby	5	1889/90	1428-1430 1697, 202																		
80	1162	Derby	5	1893	1116A-1120A	1508-1517	13″ × 20″	5′4½″	3′0″	9′0″	110	1¾″	140 PSI	3′0″	8	524	3′9½″	not quoted	19.3.1	22.19.3	400	8 cwt	1116A class. Built without cabs.
	1534	Derby	5	1897	2359-2360 1131A-1133A																		
79	1552 2517	Derby Derby	5 5	1897 1903	1134A-1138A 1139A-1143A	1518-1527	15″ × 20″	5′11″	3′9″	10′4″	141	1¾″	140/150 PSI	4′0″	10.5	761	3′9¾″/ 3′9½″	not quoted	26.12.2	30.19.2 tank half full	650	8 cwt	1134A class. Built without cabs.
N/A	3031 5528	Derby Derby	5 5	1907 1921/2	N/A	1528-1532	15″ × 22″	7′0⅛″			141	1¾″	160 PSI		10.5	767	3′10″	not quoted	27.3.3	32.16.1	650	10 cwt	1528 class. According to Radford (below) 1533-1537 were officially 'rebuilds' of older Johnson engines.

Sources: Johnson Engines – 1903 Engine Diagram Book. Deeley Engines – 'Derby Works and Midland Locomotives', J. B. Radford 1971

Perhaps one of the most interesting features of these engines was the use of outside Walschaert's valve gear, which virtually occupied the whole space between the rear wheels and the cylinders and imparted a curiously contorted aspect to the engines when in motion! It was unheard of before 1907 for the Midland to adopt outside valve gear and this class can also claim the curious statistical distinction of being the only group of MR-owned engines to be so fitted. The only other example was the lone Lickey Banker, whilst the S & DJR 2–8–0s do not, of course, qualify as Midland. It must be considered rather unusual for such an arrangement to be adopted solely for a small tank type, but it may have had something to do with the wish to fit very large side tanks which would render conventional inside motion very inaccessible. It may, however, also have had something to do with some of the other ideas being pursued at Derby at the time – a topic we explore in Chapter 6.

The two batches always differed slightly in appearance and this even extended to their original liveries, Nos. 1528-32 appearing in lined crimson, Nos. 1533-7 in unlined black, both with 14 inch numerals centred on the side. We illustrated a red one at *Plate 65* of Volume 1 but this red livery did not survive the first repaint and all were black when the LMS got them. During Midland days, as was customary for most MR tank engines in the Deeley livery, they ran without company markings on the side tanks – and this seems probably to have been true for most of them in the LMS period until c.1928, after which they received standard post-1927 LMS insignia.

Virtually all the differences between the batches were purely cosmetic and the most obvious of these was the treatment of the panel riveting. The 1907 engines had a flush finish whereas the later engines displayed a multiplicity of visible rivets. There were, however, sundry other slight variations. The handrails to the cab opening were 'flush' with the side panelling on the first batch but mounted 'outside' the tank on Nos. 1533-7; the rear footstep support plates had a straight rear edge on Nos. 1528-32 but were symmetrically shaped on the later engines, and there was no cut-out access opening for the radius rod/valve spindle joint on the first series. There were also several different patterns of stove-pipe chimneys – at least three and probably four (see pictures), the precise reason for which we cannot fathom. Perhaps a reader can help.

Plates 92 to 100. Engine No. 41528 in later years. One of the writers chanced upon this engine at Staveley in 1964 and took a number of pictures, of which this is a selection, viz., front view, left tank side, left and right tank tops, tank filler, rear right-hand side, valve gear, cab interior, cabside and rear. *R. J. Essery*

Plate 101. Pictures of S & W locos during S & W ownership are rare but we are able to feature this view of *Friar Tuck* at Berkeley Road station prior to working back to the Severn and Wye system via the Midland branch to Sharpness. Built in 1870 by Avonside of Bristol, this engine was transferred to the Midland Railway in 1895, becoming No. 1122A. In 1907 it became No. 1605 and as such it was to continue in service until withdrawn in 1911. We featured two views of this engine in Volume 1 and they are worthy of comparison with this original condition picture.
Authors' Collection

CHAPTER FOUR

NON-JOHNSON 0–6–0T CLASSES

Plate 102. A close-up of *Friar Tuck* at Berkeley Road taken at the same time as the view featured in *Plate 101.* *Authors' Collection*

IN this and the succeeding chapter, we deal mostly with the 0–6–0Ts which came to the LMS in 1923.

Although it would have been possible to put them all together, it seems better, on balance, to allocate a separate chapter to encompass the handful of non-Johnson designs with this wheel arrangement. In this group we make one exception to our 'survived to the LMS' rule by including all the locomotives taken over from the Severn & Wye in 1895, which did not, in fact, reach the LMS. It seemed tidier this way.

EX–S&W LOCOMOTIVES

The story of the Severn & Wye is both a long and complex one, but fortunately the history of this line has been well documented by the authors Ian Pope, Bob How and Paul Karau whose *Severn & Wye Railway, Vols. 1-3* have been published by Wild Swan. To those readers who are interested in the story of this line, we would recommend that they read these volumes, whose existence renders it unnecessary for us to go into any great depth when dealing with the history of the railway. Nevertheless, some brief background information would not be out of place.

It began as the 'Lydney & Lydbrook Railway', a horse-operated tramway first incorporated by an Act of Parliament in 1809. The early years were fraught with difficulty and, whilst it is outside the scope of this volume, it should be mentioned that many years were to pass before the Severn & Wye moved from tramway to railway status. Locomotives appeared in 1868, at first to broad gauge, but with a view to their early conversion to standard gauge, which took place in 1872.

Suffice to say that the Severn & Wye struggled on, but in the end the Great Western and the Midland Railway undertook jointly to purchase the lines, and on 1st July 1894 the Severn & Wye and Severn Bridge Railway was jointly vested in the Great Western and Midland Railways. A joint committee was set up to administer this concern and the MR became responsible for the maintenance of both the locomotives and rolling stock. This arrangement lasted for but a short period, and in 1895 the GWR proposal that the parent companies should provide new locomotives and rolling stock was adopted and the existing stock of engines, carriages and goods wagons was valued and divided equally between the two companies. Those which went to the Midland were eventually dispersed throughout the system.

Before describing the locomotives which came to the Midland, it is worth noting that we illustrated the left-hand side of No. 1122A (*Plates 66/67*) and both sides of No.

Plate 103. We featured a left-hand side view of No. 1606 in *LMS Locomotives Volume 4* and here we show it as No. 1124A. Originally *Sharpness*, it was an 1880 Vulcan Foundry locomotive which, as No. 1606, was to last in service until January 1924. It is difficult to be sure if this engine is in plain crimson or locomotive brown livery, but there certainly is no evidence of any lining whatsoever.

Authors' Collection

TABLE 3 – NON JOHNSON 0-6-0T CLASSES

1903 Diagram Page No.	Order No. or Class	Built by	Quantity Built	Date of Building	Pre 1907 Numbers	1907 Renumbering	Cylinders	BOILER					Working Pressure	FIREBOX		Total Heating Surface in Sq Ft	WHEELS		ENGINE WEIGHT		Water Capacity in Gallons	Coal Capacity	REMARKS
								Centre Line	Diameter	Length	Tubes	Diameter		Length	Grate Area in Sq Ft		Driving	Tyres	Empty	Loaded			
66	Beyers	Beyer Peacock	10	1871	880A-889A	1610-1619	17″ × 24″	10′6″	4′2″	10′0″	213	1¾″	140 PSI	5′0″	14.5	1115	4′2½″	2¾″	32.5.2	40.5.1	950	24 cwt	880 class. Originally built with cut down boiler mounting etc.
75	Friar Tuck	Avonside	1	1870	1122A	1605	16″ × 24″	not quoted	4′2″	10′0″	213	1¾″	140 PSI	5′0″	14.5	1115	4′3″	not quoted	34.6.2	41.9.3	845	24 cwt	**Ex Severn and Wye Locomotives.** As Rebuilt by the MR.
76	Little John	Fletcher Jennings	1	1874	1123A	–	16″ × 24″	not quoted	4′1″	9′9¼″	191	1¾″	140 PSI	4′6⅞″	12.7	965.79	4′0″	not quoted	31.17.1	39.10.1	920	not quoted	Withdrawn 1905 – as rebuilt at Lydney by S. & W.
77	Sharp-ness	Vulcan	1	1880	1124A	1606	17″ × 24″	not quoted	4′1″	9′3″	193	1¾″	140 PSI	4′8″	13.5	948.4	4′3″	not quoted	32.4.3	39.17.3	896	not quoted	As built.
78	Sabrina Forester	Vulcan	1 1	1882 1886	1125A 1126A	1607 1608	16½″ × 24″	not quoted	4′2″	10′0″	213	1¾″	140 PSI	5′0″	14.5	1115	4′3″	not quoted	32.4.1	39.8.0	845	not quoted	As rebuilt by MR.

Source: 1903 Engine Diagram Book

1123A (*Plates 68/69*) in Volume 1 of this series. In addition, we featured No. 1606 at *Plate 219* in Volume 4 of *An Illustrated History of LMS Locomotives* (Silver Link Publishing).

THE SEVERN & WYE LOCOMOTIVES TO THE MIDLAND RAILWAY IN 1895

0–6–0T *Robin Hood* – Built in 1868 by Fletcher Jennings. Allocated MR No. 1121A but not carried. The locomotive was withdrawn in 1895.

0–6–0T *Friar Tuck* – Built 1870 by Avonside Engine Co., became MR No. 1122A. Renumbered 1605 in 1907. Withdrawn in 1911.

0–6–0T *Little John* – Built 1874 by Fletcher Jennings. Became MR No. 1123A. Withdrawn in 1905.

0–6–0T *Sharpness* – Built 1880 by Vulcan Foundry. Became MR No. 1124A. Renumbered 1606 in 1907. Withdrawn in 1924.

0–6–0T *Sabrina* – Built by Vulcan Foundry 1882. Became MR No. 1125A. Renumbered 1607 in 1907. Withdrawn in 1920.

0–6–0T *Forester* – Built by Vulcan Foundry 1886. Became MR No. 1126A. Renumbered 1608 in 1907. Withdrawn in 1924.

Upon becoming Midland Railway locomotives, all the names were removed.

By the time these engines had been in Midland service for a few years, the inside cylinder engines were beginning to take on quite distinctively Johnson characteristics and indeed, could quite easily be mistaken, at first glance, for the genuine Johnson breed. In addition, we presume that at least Nos. 1606-08 acquired dished Deeley smokebox doors and chimneys well before the dates of withdrawal.

Plate 104. This picture should have been *Plate 70* in Volume 1. Regrettably, the pictures were transposed at the 'making up' stage, see Errata to Volume 1 published in Volume 2. This locomotive as illustrated was originally Severn & Wye *Sabrina* and was built by the Vulcan Foundry in 1882. Becoming Midland Railway No. 1125A in 1895, it was to become No. 1607 in 1907 and was withdrawn in 1920.

Authors' Collection

Plate 105. This right-hand side view of ex Severn & Wye Railway *Forester* in lined crimson lake livery illustrates a locomotive built by the Vulcan Foundry in 1886. Note the similarity to the 'A' class engines described in Chapter 5. It was to become MR No. 1126A as illustrated and in 1907 it was renumbered 1608. Withdrawal was in 1924.

National Railway Museum

Plate 106. This photograph illustrates the first of the class in original condition. *National Railway Museum*

Plate 106A. 0–6–0T No. 882 in its original condition. When built they were in green livery with reduced boiler mountings as illustrated. Note the arrangement of the Salter safety valves, in front of the dome. Becoming No. 882A in 1890 and No. 1612 in 1907, it was to survive until 1926. We illustrated this locomotive as No. 882A in Volume 1 at *Plate 220.*
Authors' Collection

880 CLASS

In 1871 Beyer Peacock constructed ten 0–6–0T engines to Kirtley's design and they were built to a restricted loading gauge of 10 ft. 6 in. height in order to work to Midland Railway goods stations in the East London area. With inside frames, they represented a departure from Kirtley's principle of double frames, the usual hallmark of his designs. As far as we know, they were always in the London district and, according to one source, they were always allocated to Kentish Town shed.

When constructed, they were built with a spectacle plate only (see *Plate 106A*), but later on, a less open or 'half' cab was added during the Johnson period and at the same time they received 'A' class boilers. In addition, when built, the Salter safety valves were mounted onto a low dome with the pillars attached to the boiler sides at approximately 45 degrees to the boiler centre-line. In 1890 they were all placed on the duplicate list as 880A, etc.

Although quite properly attributed to Kirtley, this group of engines, like many others made by this celebrated manufacturer, always carried a degree of Beyer-Peacock styling. The riveted tanks and lack of footplate angle were distinctly 'un-Midland' and even when the MR had fitted a shallow footplate angle ahead of the side tanks and given them a full array of 'Derby' fittings, the engines still looked slightly alien. In this respect they had something in common with the Beyer Peacock built 0–4–4Ts (Chapter 1) and 4–4–0Ts (Vol. 6).

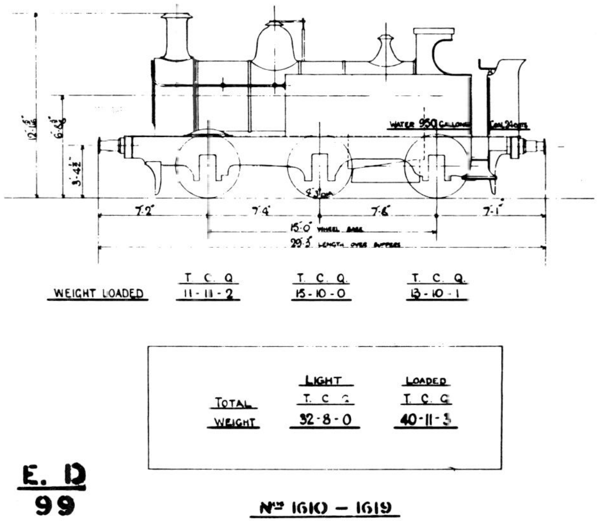

Fig. 15. ED 99 was the Midland Railway 1910 Engine Diagram for this series of locomotives, Nos. 1610-1619.
National Railway Museum

Summary

Built by Beyer Peacock & Co. in 1871. Original Midland Railway numbers 880-889. Renumbered 880A-889A in 1890. Renumbered in 1907, becoming 1610-1619. All to the LMS in 1923. Class extinct in 1927. Allocated to Engine Diagram 99 in 1910.

The Midland Railway owned a number of 'non-Johnson' tank engines, both passenger and freight, and, because many never even survived to be renumbered in 1907, it was felt that the remainder which did not reach the LMS should all be included within Volume 6. A number of these locomotives were illustrated in Volume 1 (*Plates 62, 71, 72, 74, 150*) but a more complete story will be found in the final volume of this series.

Plate 107. This view of No. 885A at Stratford in 1902 shows an example of the 'decorated' London style of livery discussed fully in Volume 1, e.g. *Plates 224-6* where indeed we illustrate another view of this locomotive. An earlier view of the engine is below at *Plate 108.*
Authors' Collection

Plate 108. No. 885A in crimson lake livery after rebuilding with conventional height chimney but still with a low dome. The lining is limited, on the tank side panel and on the end. There appears to be no lining on the wheels but there could be on the bosses. However, below the platform the footstep supports and sandboxes are lined. Becoming No. 1615 in 1907, it was to last until 1925 when it was withdrawn from service. Note that the Salter valves are still set at 45 degrees, even with the new taller chimney. We illustrated this locomotive after rebuilding with a cab at *Plate 224*, Volume 1.
W. T. Stubbs

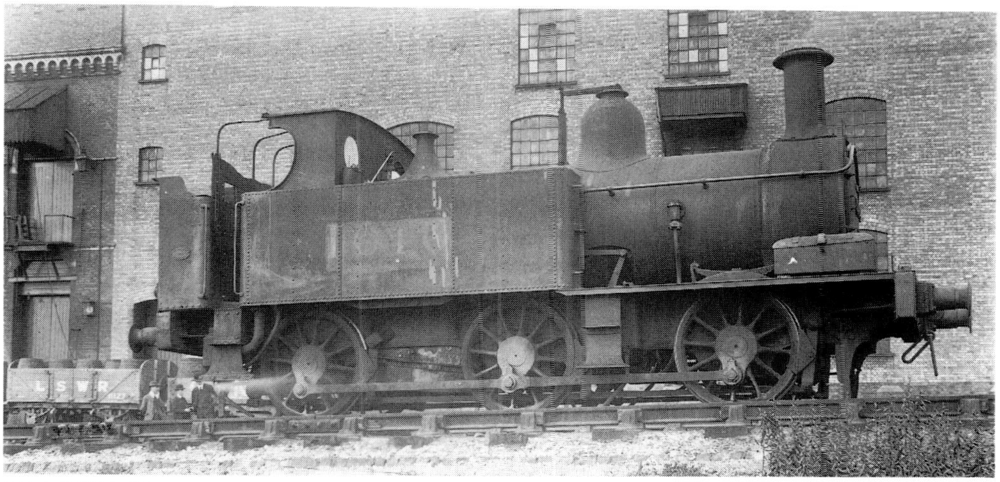

Plate 110. Old No. 888 is seen here as No. 1618 in its final years when running in black livery. It was withdrawn in 1925. *Authors' Collection*

Plates 109 & 111. Nos. 1610 and 1619 in plain black livery. In these views we see the first and last of the '880' class locomotives during their final years. Note on No. 1610 the toolbox at the front end of the platform and the rails attached to the cab which enabled a tarpaulin sheet to be used. From practical experience, one of us knows how difficult it would have been to work with a sheet attached to the 'half cab' without something to lift it up and give more 'footplate space'. Compared with No. 1619, No. 1610 has a continuous handrail with a flat smokebox, whereas No. 1619 has separate handrails with a dished smokebox door. Note in both cases the later addition of leading footsteps, a vertical handrail at the front of, and a shallow footplate angle ahead of, the side tanks. *Authors' Collection and Collection Bernard Mathews*

Plate 112. No. 1116 in works grey and original condition. Note the wing plates, later to be removed. In addition, attention is drawn to the wooden brake blocks, together with the early type of lubricator at the base of the smokebox and shackle coupling at the front. Comparison of this picture with those taken at a later date will also reveal that the plain one-piece cast chimney has replaced the built-up chimney seen in this view. Other changes to be noted are evident in the shape of the dome and rear safety valve covers. Built in 1875, No. 1116 remained on the capital list, becoming No. 1634 in 1907, withdrawal taking place in 1927.

National Railway Museum

CHAPTER FIVE

THE JOHNSON 0-6-0 TANKS

WE now turn to the large series of 0—6—0Ts built by Johnson between 1874 and 1902 which eventually totalled 340 machines (1907 Nos. 1620-1959). In later years these were usually regarded as falling into two groups only, designated by power class. On this basis most were Class 1 engines and only the last sixty were of the Class 3 type (Nos. 1900-59).

However, in Midland days, the Class 1 engines actually came in three quite distinct categories (or 'classes' if you prefer). There were indeed many similarities between them but we have elected to follow the formal Midland breakdown and treat them as three series. *Plates 112-118* illustrate the series 'as built' and variations thereof. They did, of course, all become Class 1/1F in due course. The term 'half cab' has been used widely in recent years, but the more proper term is 'open cab' to denote the version which did not have an overall roof between front spectacle plate and bunker. However, we doubt if this will have much effect on popular usage!

The story of the Johnson 0—6—0Ts begins with the construction of forty locomotives between 1874-1876 by Neilsons & Vulcans and known as the 'A' or '1102' class. When built, they were fitted with the earlier style of Johnson dome and safety valves. They were, unlike many later locomotives of this series, fitted with overall cabs from new.

They were followed by the '1377' class which began to enter service in 1878 and, while some sources suggest that there were 185 engines in the '1377' class (1907 Nos. 1660-1844), by 1903, according to the Engine Diagram Book published in that year, the Midland had allocated these locomotives onto four separate diagrams. We have not divided up this group in a similar manner for in truth, apart from the '1552' class (see page 102), there was little difference between them all, apart from the fact that five of the locomotives were built new with full cabs and a number were later so fitted.

The construction of this '1377' series of 0—6—0T tank engines continued until 1892, after which there was a pause, and when construction commenced again some three years later, the principal difference was a longer wheelbase with a 6 in. increase and they were all built with overall cabs.

Plate 113. No. 1390 was built in 1878 and is seen here in green livery. Note the Midland Railway builders' plate on the bunker side. Renumbered No. 1673 in 1907, in 1912 this locomotive received a closed cab. It remained in service until the end of 1930. A further Midland Railway pre-1907 picture of this locomotive appears at *Plate 130*, page 85. *Collection Bernard Mathews*

Plate 114. No. 1557 was built in 1882 with cut-down boiler mountings and reduced height cab when compared with the '1377' class, and is seen here in this condition in works grey livery. Becoming No. 1715 in 1907, it was to be withdrawn in 1932.

Collection Bernard Mathews

Plate 115. This is an official view of No. 1124 taken c.1903 and it should be noted that the MR photographic studio, when painting out the unwanted background detail, has removed the lamp irons! Seen here in lined crimson lake livery, No. 1124 was built at Derby in 1895. Becoming No. 1848 in 1907, it was an early withdrawal, being taken out of service by the LMS in 1932. *National Railway Museum*

Plate 116. This view of No. 2252 illustrates one of the series of five locomotives built with a somewhat different cab with a semi-open back. No. 2252 was to become No. 1859 and in due course No. 41859 before withdrawal by British Railways in 1955. Compare with *Plate 180.*
National Railway Museum

Plate 117. Built as No. 2742, this locomotive became No. 1921 in 1907. In 1934 it became LMS No. 7221 and a Belpaire boiler was not fitted until 1940. Withdrawal as British Railways No. 47221 was in 1961. A further view of this engine will be found at *Plate 202.*
Collection Bernard Mathews

Plate 118. No. 1934 as reboilered in 1919 by the Midland Railway. This photographic grey picture is misleading insofar as it suggests the locomotive was to be painted in lined crimson lake livery, whereas it entered traffic in plain black livery. Originally No. 2755, it was built in 1902 and became No. 7234 as part of the LMS 1934 renumbering scheme. It was withdrawn from service in 1958 as British Railways No. 47234.

British Railways

Plate 119. No. 1136 when photographed at Durran Hill, carried a very elaborate crimson lake livery, in fact a form of 'London Style'. Note the inner 'panel' on both the tank and bunker sides, a black line with yellow lining on both sides. This style, whilst not unique, is the only example we have recorded within this particular class of locomotives. No. 1136 was to become 1654 in 1907 and was withdrawn from service in 1928.
Authors' Collection

They were to be known as the '1121' class (1907 Nos. 1845-1899).

The next change came in 1899 when a much enlarged 0–6–0T with an 8 ft. x 8 ft. 6 in. wheelbase entered service. A total of sixty engines were built by Vulcan, to be known as the S & U or the '2441' class. Later, when the first locomotives were rebuilt with Belpaire boilers, they became the basis of the LMS standard Class 3 0–6–0Ts built in considerable numbers for shunting and local goods working between 1924 and 1931. Originally numbered 1900-1959 (following the 1907 renumbering), they were to be the final 0–6–0Ts to be built by the company.

From this point onwards we shall consider all these engines separately by the various classes defined above.

'A' OR 1102 CLASS

The 'A' or '1102' class 0–6–0Ts were the first new Johnson design to be built by the Midland Railway, fulfilling an urgent need for locomotives of that type. It was suggested by Ahrons that it was the needs of the newly acquired Swansea Vale line and its associated branches that prompted the construction of this class, and, since the first twenty to be built were put to work on these lines and members of the class remained there for many years, this seems very likely. They were built with all-over cabs although No. 1139 was altered to an open back variety (see *Plate 121*) and No. 1644 had the rear spectacle plate removed (*Plate 127*). The exact date of these conversions (or the reason why) is unknown to the authors and there may have been other cab variations; further information would be welcome. These locomotives were to remain in this condition for the rest of their existence.

Other changes to be noted were that the position and size of toolboxes varied with this class and, whereas two coal rails were usual, a picture exists which shows No. 2255 with three, an attempt, no doubt, to increase the very limited coal capacity of these engines (see *Table 6*). There may have been others.

When first built, they lacked forward steps, but these were fitted after 1903 when additional vertical handrails also appeared on the end of the side tanks. As befits this early Johnson class, the original brake hangers were later altered to a more straight type (see pictures), and of course for the first ten or so years they ran in green before carrying the red livery. They also had wing plates when built but this 'un-Midland' feature was removed at an early date. Other detail variations (boiler mountings and angle iron cut-aways) are dealt with in the photo captions.

Summary

Built by Neilson & Co. 1874-1875 (1102-1126) and Vulcan Foundry 1875-1876 (1127-1141). In 1891 Nos. 1102-1115 were renumbered in the duplicate list as 1102A-1115A. In 1895 Nos. 1121-1130 became Nos. 1125A-1130A on the duplicate list and later in the same year Nos. 1121A-1126A were altered to 2253-2258.

The Midland Railway 1907 numbers were 1620-1659. All to the LMS except No. 1628. All were built with enclosed cabs. Class extinct 1932.

Allocated to Engine Diagram 100 in 1910. It should be noted that in 1903 two separate diagrams (see *Table 6*) were in use and these diagrams were for either capital stock or duplicated stock locomotives.

Plate 120. No. 1103A at Brecon in full crimson lake livery. Built as No. 1103 and becoming 1103A in 1891, it lasted until withdrawal in 1928 as LMS No. 1621. Note the jack on the platform by the smokebox, the toolbox on the tanktop and the brake hangers. A later style of brake hanger will be seen on the post-1907 plates. Close examination of the picture also shows a footplate full of coal — a case of over-coaling or perhaps preparation for a long turn of duty. Certainly the next series, the '1377' class, almost doubled the coal capacity.

Collection Bernard Mathews

Plate 121. No. 1139 at Normanton in October 1900. Built in 1876, this locomotive was to become No. 1657 in 1907 and was withdrawn in 1930 without further change to the cab. It is interesting to note that this locomotive has had the rear of its cab removed. There is no evidence of any lining anywhere but the top of the splasher appears to be a darker colour, which suggests that No. 1139 is in locomotive brown livery.

Collection Ken Nunn

Plate 122. No. 1128A illustrates a Vulcan Foundry-built locomotive photographed c.1903 in lined crimson lake livery. When compared with *Plates 119 & 120*, the later type of smaller brass safety valve cover will be noted. In addition, No. 1128A has forward front footsteps and handrail at the ends of the side tanks. Other differences are in the shape of the brake hangers and the cut-away of the angle iron or valance around the rear steps. Built in 1875, it became No. 1128A in 1895 and No. 1646 in 1907. Withdrawal by the LMS took place in 1929.

National Railway Museum

Plate 123. No. 1135, probably photographed c.1904, displays no evidence of lining whatsoever. It is almost certainly an example of locomotive brown livery or a very dirty red livery. Compared with *Plates 119 & 120*, this picture illustrates a locomotive with side steps forward of the tank sides, a feature also shared with No. 1128A. Note also the longer toolbox on the tanktop when compared with No. 1103A. By the LMS period the toolbox was on the running plate to the left of the smokebox. In 1907 No. 1135 became No. 1653 and was withdrawn in 1931. *National Railway Museum*

Plate 124. This picture of No. 1111 was taken in 1903 but on the original print it can be seen that the 'A' has been blanked out for the purpose of the photograph. No. 1111A was used as the official picture in the 1903 Engine Diagram Book, by which date it was on the duplicate list, hence the disguise. This view should be compared with No. 1116 in *Plate 112* which illustrates the 'as built' condition. Note the changes which have taken place: removal of the wing plate, one-piece chimney, new dome cover, three-link couplings and, of course, the fitting of cast iron brake shoes. *National Railway Museum*

Plate 125. No. 1632 in close-up. This is an alternative view of the same locomotive shown in *Plate 100* in Volume 1, showing the arrangement of the end train pipes and vacuum control regulator.
National Railway Museum

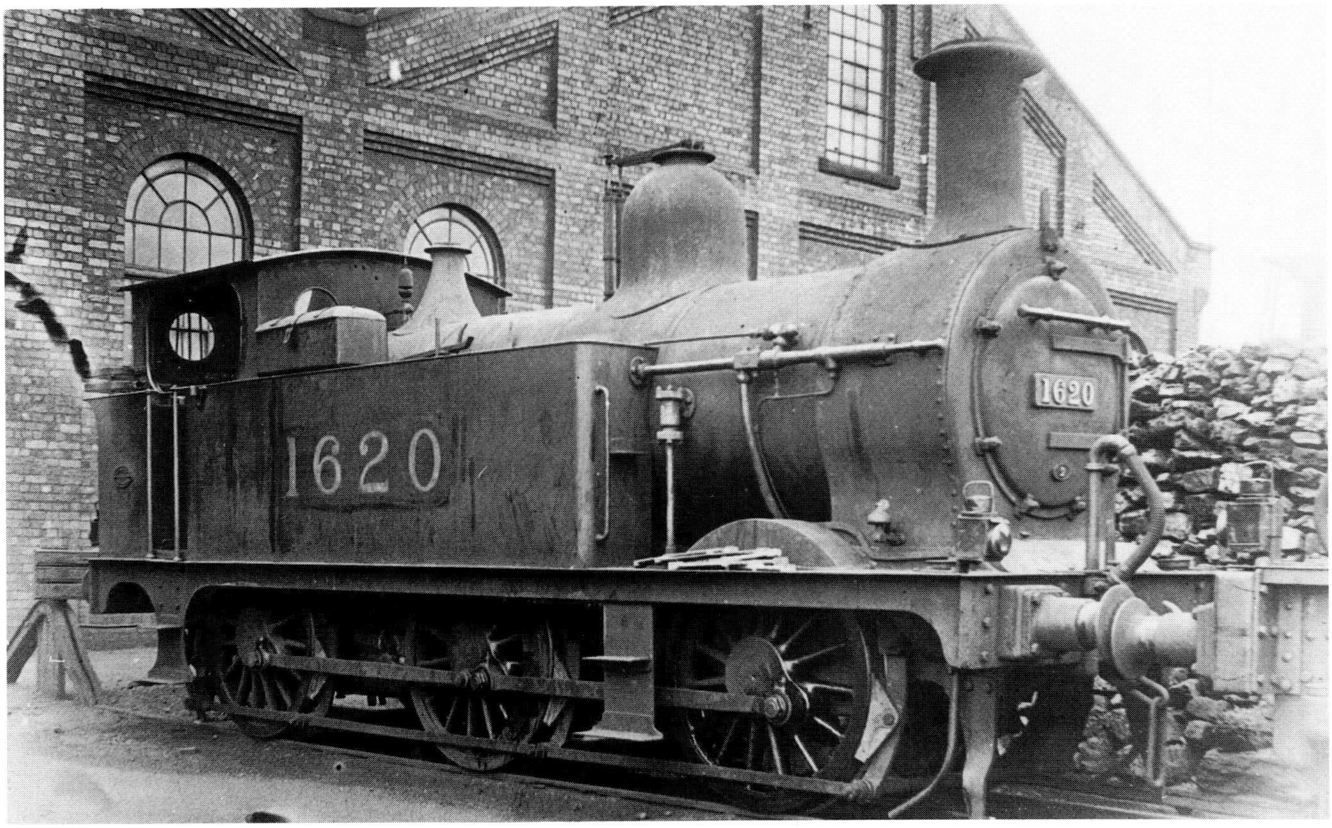

Plate 126. The pioneer member of the class, No. 1102, as No. 1620, is illustrated in this picture when at Burton engine shed in June 1924. Note the toolbox on the top of the tank and the footstep fitted c.1903 forward of the tank. This locomotive was withdrawn in 1928.
Authors' Collection

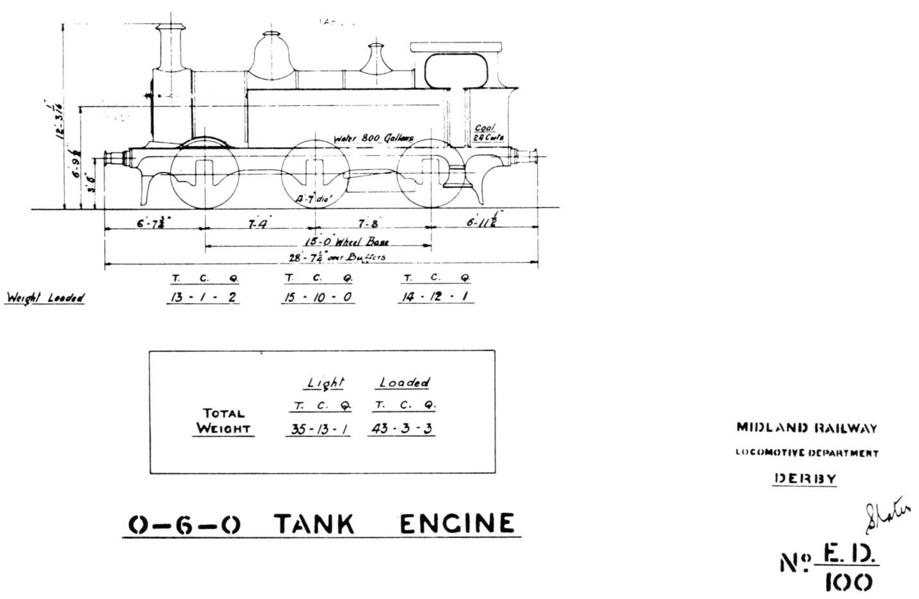

Fig. 16. Engine Diagram 100. This diagram was issued in 1910 by the Midland Railway and referred to this series of locomotives.
Authors' Collection

Plates 127 & 128. No. 1644, originally No. 1126, which ran as No. 2258 from 1895 until 1907, is shown here at Derby in June 1926 in LMS pre-1928 freight livery. By now the continuous handrail has been replaced and the forward footstep has been fitted. The most interesting feature of this locomotive is the absence of the rear cab spectacle plate, the only example we have found within the class. The five Sharp Stewart-built 'Class Q' (see page 107 & *Table 6*) were also built without a rear spectacle plate and, of course, No. 1657, shown as No. 1139 in *Plate 121*, has the entire rear of the cab removed. We would welcome further details regarding the modifications. No. 1644 was withdrawn from service in 1932. *Authors' Collection*
H. C. Casserley

Plate 129. This view shows No. 1630 at Peterborough in 1927 and illustrates a locomotive equipped with a train pipe and thus able to work passenger trains, not every member of the class was so fitted. *Authors' Collection*

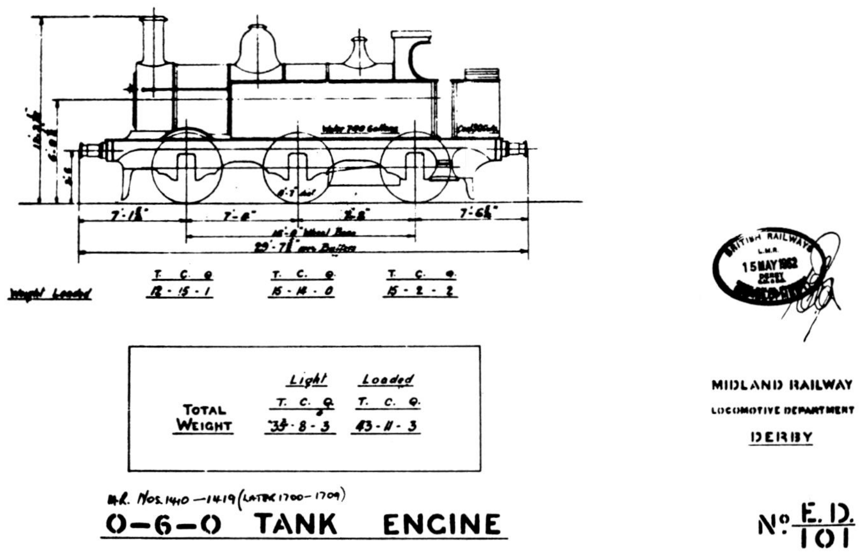

Fig. 17. Engine Diagram 101 appears to cover the series which became Nos. 1700-1709 (and probably also Nos. 1805-1814). We believe that this diagram shows a full height cab but is probably incorrectly dimensioned.
Authors' Collection

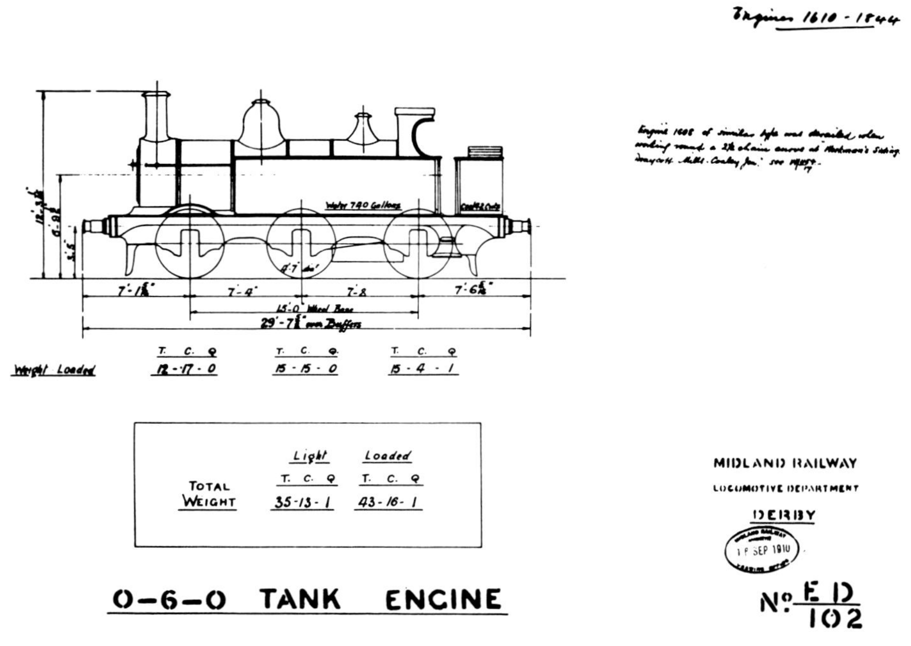

Fig. 18. Engine Diagram 102 is of the 'typical' variety and it is claimed that it encompasses all the engines numbered between 1610 and 1844 but it may be taken as referring to the 'old 1377' class.
Authors' Collection

Plate 130. An earlier view of the engine, when in green livery, will be found at *Plate 113*, page 73. Here we see lined red livery and one-piece cast chimney and coal rails, together with the later style of safety valve and steam dome. *Authors' Collection*

1377 CLASS

The second Johnson design of goods tank engines began to enter service in 1878 when the locomotives built to order No. 204 arrived on the scene. This first batch, Nos. 1377-1386, marked the beginning of a series of six-coupled tank engines intended principally for shunting work. Therefore it seems possible that the 'closed cab' version which preceded them was perhaps regarded as a rather superior form, suitable for passenger working, where its closed cab would give greater protection for the crew (in either direction) when running at the expected higher speeds of a passenger train. The open cab version was probably considered to afford easier 'look out' in the shunting yards and the slower speeds would not make its exposed footplate quite so unbearable; in any case it was no worse, in absolute terms, than a typical Johnson tender engine which was expected to spend its life on the main line although admittedly tender engines were turned where possible.

It is even possible that the later fitting of closed cabs had something to do with the increased possibility of their being called upon to work 'out on the line' rather than in the yards. Most authorities consider that the entire series, which in 1907 became 1660-1844, were one class but, as will be seen, the Midland Railway in 1903 did not take this view and divided them between pages 50, 51, 52 and 53 of the Engine Diagram Book, but the reasons for this action were not too clear (see *Table 6*). By 1910 we believe that the Engine Diagrams officially allocated to this series were ED 101 for 1700-1709 (plus others?) and ED 102 for the entire series as 1660-1844!

With the exception of engines Nos. 218-219, 1397-1399 (1907 Nos. 1725-1729) which were built new with enclosed cabs and vacuum brakes for service on the Keighley to Oxenhope branch, all other locomotives were built with open cabs but many were later fitted with closed cabs.

According to one reliable source (*The History of 1708 and the Midland Open Cab 0–6–0 Tanks* by S. Summerson, 1979) it is recorded that when built, with the exception of the five locomotives mentioned, all engines were also built as 'steam brake only'. Later, many of the open cab engines were also vacuum-fitted to enable them to shunt vacuum-braked stock. Apart from their obvious use on carriage shunting or on branch passenger duties, there was also the need to be able to 'blow up' or create the vacuum on the 'fitted' portion of express goods trains prior to the arrival of the train engines at the marshalling yards and major goods depots.

In addition a number of locomotives fitted with end train pipes were also equipped with carriage-warming apparatus which began to appear from c.1900 onwards.

Plate 131. No. 1424 is seen here in full crimson lake livery as running c.1900. Becoming No. 1696 in 1907, it was withdrawn in 1936. Note the absence of toolboxes on the platform.
Authors' Collection

Fig. 19. This drawing illustrates the Vulcan-built 0–6–0Ts, known as 'Class N' in their original condition. Originally MR Nos. 1993-2012, they became Nos. 1825-1844 in 1907. *P. J. Truman*

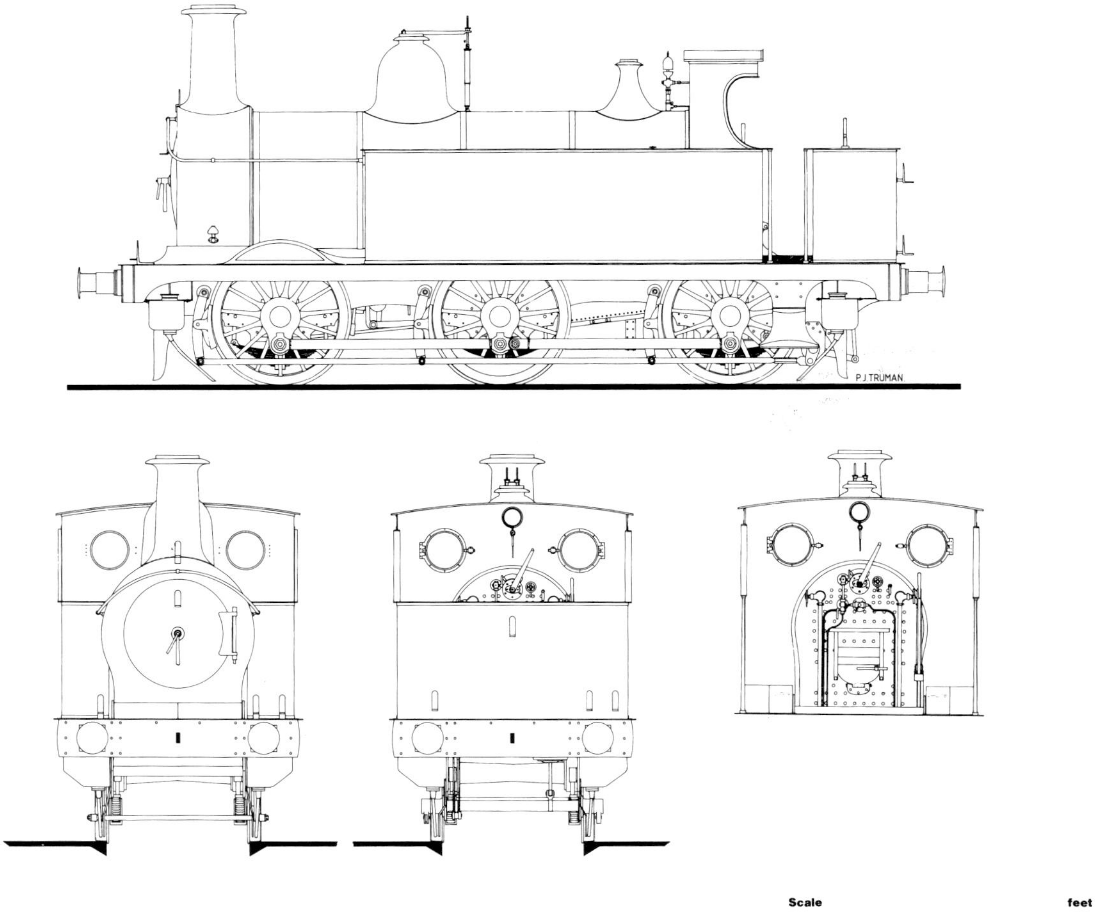

Commencing in 1910, a number of locomotives received new frames, and rebuilding with G5 Belpaire boilers commenced in 1924 with No. 1741. This programme continued until 1930 when a downturn in traffic led to its abandonment. By this date 88 locomotives had been so equipped. Rebuilding with Belpaire G5 boilers began again during the Second World War and this programme continued until 1961 and with the rebuilding of No. 41835, a total of 105 engines had been converted to Belpaire boiler form.

Coal Rails

It would seem that the 0–6–0Ts first entered traffic without coal rails, although these were added from the 1890s. Whilst two was the usual number, three and four coal rails were not unknown and Table 5 sets out all those locomotives running with additional coal rails which are known to the authors. Whilst on the subject of coal rails and coal capacity, it should be noted that the information given in *Table 6* shows them all to be of 42 cwt capacity. The information used to compile this table was dated 1903.

Cabs

We have identified five versions which can be summarised as follows. Apart from type C1, first fitted to engines Nos. 218/219, 1397-1399, we cannot say which design came next, but *Plates 138/147/149/151/153* illustrate the styles. Locomotives known to have been fitted with these different cabs are listed in *Table 4*, with dates where known.

The cabs fall into two distinct styles and may be summarised as having either 'vertical' cut-aways or 'curved Johnson style' cut-aways, as will be seen from the pictures. C1 and C2 form one group, namely with vertical cut-aways, while C3, C4 and C5 are the second group described as curved Johnson style. We know that style C1 was the first design using two very narrow panels as side sheets, front and rear, both of equal width with a pronounced curved top. No. 218 (*Plate 138*) illustrates this style. C2 followed the style of C1 except that the side sheets were wider and No. 1676 (*Plate 153*) clearly illustrates this design, the confirmed examples of which exceed any other style.

The second group contained an example where the cut-out was more vertical than curved, but where the wide

Plate 132. No. 1347 (which was to become No. 1680 in 1907 and was to last until 1932) is seen here fitted with a rear weatherboard for passenger train working prior to achieving a 'C1' style cab. This picture displays the full crimson lake livery as applied to this class of locomotive.
Courtesy Keighley & Worth Valley Railway

Plate 133. No. 1350 was built at Derby in 1879 and is seen here as running during the early years of this century. Service was to continue until 1932 but in 1907 it was to become No. 1683. *National Railway Museum*

front side sheet was more in keeping with what we have chosen to call the 'curved Johnson style', so we have placed type C4 in this second group (see No. 1730 *Plate 149*). Type C3 was similar but with a curved cut-out to the rear side sheet. We have only been able to identify one example, No. 1769 (*Plate 147*). Type C5, exemplified by No. 1669 (*Plate 151*) is the final style of cab to be identified. It has the front side sheet of the open cab engines with the wider rear side sheet of C2.

TABLE 4
'1377' Class Cab Variations — Confirmed Pictures

C1	C2	C3	C4		C5	
1394 (1677)	1676	1769	1730		1665	
1678	1767		1734	Believed fitted 1906	1666	
1680	1768		1735		1667	
218 (1725)	1776		1736		1668	
1726	1777				1669	Believed fitted in 1912
1727	1778				1670	
1728	1779				1672	
1729	1816				1673	
1420 (1692)	1817				1674	
	1818					
	1819					
	1820					
	1822					
	1823					
	1824					
	1833					
	1834					

Whilst we believe that the addition of enclosed cabs may have been intended to coincide with the fitting of vacuum brakes, we cannot be certain (1907 Nos. 1725-1729 were built with enclosed cabs; all other examples of the feature were fitted later). Moreover, as the years passed by, photographic evidence exists of enclosed cab engines without vacuum brakes and, of course, open cab engines with them, so there would seem to be no clearly defined pattern.

Finally, examples of coal rail variations from the normal two coal rail arrangement are included in Table 5.

TABLE 5
'1377' Class Coal Rail Variations

Three Coal Rails	*Four Coal rails*
215 (1723)	1669
1724	1670
1769	1676

Whilst a final series of twenty locomotives was built by Vulcan in 1892 and was referred to as the 'N' class, they were really part of the '1377' class and their original Midland Railway numbers were 1993-2012. In 1907 they were renumbered 1825-1844 and as such concluded the building of this group of locomotives. There was, however, a variation which we now need to consider: two orders for engines with cut down boiler mountings. These were known as the '1552' class.

Plates 134 & 135. These two views of the same locomotive show No. 1973 which became No 1786 in 1907. Withdrawal was in 1932. When photographed as No. 1973 it was in simplified crimson lake livery, whereas when photographed as No. 1786 it was in plain black. By this date a temporary additional cab roof had been fitted. *Authors' Collection and Bernard Mathews Collection*

Plate 136. Three coal rails round the bunker was a little unusual but the arrangement is seen here in this view of No. 215 taken c.1905. In lined crimson lake livery, it also shows end train pipes and the old style of double brake hangers, later to be replaced by single style (see pictures). Also in this view we have a locomotive which has an unusual arrangement to the front spectacle plate. Note the vertical beading arrangement. No. 215 was built in 1883 and became No. 1723 in 1907. Withdrawal was in 1930. *National Railway Museum*

Plate 137. A very early conversion to enclosed cab status was No. 1394, which is seen in this photograph taken c.1905. Built in 1878, it was to become No. 1677 in 1907, and in its c.1927 condition is featured in *Plate 141* where its final history is given. This picture shows the lined crimson lake livery. *Authors' Collection*

Plate 138. This splendid works grey picture of No. 218 illustrates a locomotive built in 1883 to work passenger trains, and at first it was employed upon the Keighley to Oxenhope line, hence the enclosed cab and end train pipes. No. 218 was to become No. 1725 in 1907 and No. 41725 following Nationalisation. Withdrawal was in 1955. Note the double curved brake hangers. This style was associated with the earlier Johnson designs – later the brake hanger arrangement was a single hanger, and a rather straighter arrangement. This style is to be seen in *Plate 149.* *National Railway Museum*

Plate 139. The series which were to become Nos. 1730-59 were all built with open cabs, and this rear view of No. 1741, taken at Bournville in August 1919, shows a locomotive in plain black Midland livery. Originally No. 1091, this locomotive is recorded as receiving a Belpaire boiler before withdrawal which occurred at the end of 1932.
W. L. Good

Plate 140. Readers can compare two contrasting cab views showing No. 1758 at *Plate 106* in Vol. 1 and No. 1756 illustrated here. No. 1756 is equipped with a control for the vacuum brake and could thus be employed upon passenger trains. This brake was operated by the handle at the bottom right-hand corner just to the right of the chalked 1756. The picture of No. 1756 is also useful insofar as it shows the Salter safety valves from the rear viewpoint. The picture of No. 1758 in Vol. 1 illustrated a locomotive which was only fitted with a steam brake controlled by the handle mounted below the steam regulator.
National Railway Museum

Plate 141. No. 1677 (old No. 1394) on passenger work at Swansea when in LMS pre-1928 black livery. Note the later position for the toolbox and the dished smokebox door with additional lamp iron. No. 1677 was withdrawn in 1931.
Collection Bernard Mathews

Plate 142. No. 1674 was built as No. 1391 and was fitted with a closed cab in 1912. It lasted until 1948 but was not renumbered by British Railways. It is seen here in plain black Midland Railway livery, c.1922. *Authors' Collection*

Plate 143. This view of No. 1670 at St. Albans illustrates old No. 1387 in almost its final condition. Note the additional coal rails. This locomotive was employed on Hemel Hempstead branch trains which may account for the requirement for additional coal capacity.
A. G. Ellis

Plate 144. The series of locomotives which became Nos. 1725-1729 were built with enclosed cabs and this picture illustrates No. 1726 at Derby in November 1949. Built as No. 219 in 1883, it was withdrawn in 1959 as 41726.

W. L. Good

Plate 145. No. 1751 in LMS plain black livery with 1C in gold letters. Note the Belpaire boiler and Ramsbottom safety valves. Built as No. 1693, it was withdrawn in 1946.

Authors' Collection

Plate 146. To illustrate a further member of works order 414 which included the five built with enclosed cabs, we have chosen this picture of old No. 210 seen here in LMS ownership as No. 1720 and fitted with a Belpaire boiler. Becoming No. 41720 following Nationalisation, the locomotive was to be withdrawn in 1956. Note the vacuum train pipe and 22B Gloucester shed plate.

Collection Bernard Mathews

Plate 147. No. 1769 was photographed at Upper Bank in June 1938. Built in 1890 as No. 1431, it was reboilered with a Belpaire boiler in 1926 having previously received a closed cab code C3 — the only example of this type we have recorded. Renumbered by British Railways as No. 41769, it was withdrawn in 1962. *Authors' Collection*

Plate 148. This illustrates No. 1769 in the same condition but from the opposite side. *Authors' Collection*

Plage 149. No. 1730, an enclosed cab locomotive photographed in LMS post-1928 livery, was built as No. 1677 in 1884 and was to be withdrawn by the LMS in the condition illustrated at the end of 1936. In this splendid ex works picture we see an enclosed cab locomotive with what we have described as a type C4 cab. Note the later type of brake hangers and the toolbox located on the left-hand side of the locomotive.
Authors' Collection

Plate 150. No. 1665 at Bedford in August 1936. Built as No. 1382, it was fitted with a closed cab in 1912 and lasted until withdrawal from service at the end of 1937.
Collection A. G. Ellis

Plate 151. A type C5 cab is seen here in this view of No. 1669 which started life as No. 1386 in 1878. No. 1669 was to survive until 1935. Note the additional coal rails and end train pipes, details associated with locomotives employed upon passenger workings. *Authors' Collection*

Plate 152. No. 1718 is seen here in LMS ownership in plain black and as such is in typical condition for the open cab round-top boilered locomotives during the 1930s period. Allocated the number 41718 by British Railways, the locomotive was withdrawn in 1948 without being renumbered and still carrying the LMS number. *Authors' Collection*

Plate 153. No. 1676 was built in 1878 as No. 1393, and renumbered in 1907. Here it is seen equipped with additional coal rails and fitted with vacuum brake (note the train end pipes). As such it is now capable of working passenger trains. *Authors' Collection*

Plate 154. We are not sure if any other members of this class ever sported a chimney of this nature; for aesthetic reasons we hope not! Photographed at Holbeck in May 1938, we see No. 1748 carrying a 20A Leeds shedplate. Built as Midland No. 1690, it was to become British Railways No. 41748 prior to withdrawal in 1957. *Collection Bernard Mathews*

Plate 155. Old No. 14 was built in 1890 and renumbered No. 1106 the following year and No. 1779 in 1907. Later it received an enclosed cab code C2 and lasted until withdrawal as British Railways No. 41779 (see *Plate 160*). Not many Class 1F 0–6–0Ts received the LMS 1936 livery but No. 1779 was one of them. It is interesting to note that when photographed at Derby in October 1938 No. 1779 had a toolbox on the platform whereas when running as No. 41779 it had been removed. *L. Hanson*

Plate 156. This view of No. 41804 shows the first stage of British Railways numbering influence, namely the retention of the letters 'LMS' while the LMS number has been increased by 40000. Built as No. 889 in 1890, this engine was to be one of the final survivors of the class, lasting until 1966 when it was withdrawn. *H. C. Casserley*

Plate 157. We illustrated this locomotive in late LMS condition at *Plate 144*; here we show it in its final British Railways condition in this picture dated March 1956.
A. G. Ellis

Plate 158. The final BR livery was with tankside emblem and small BR numbers, as seen in this picture of No. 41661. Built in 1878 as No. 1378, the second member of the class, this locomotive was to last until 1959. This view, which shows a locomotive with a Belpaire boiler, typifies the final condition of many of the open cab locomotives in their final years. *Authors' Collection*

Plate 159. The next British Railways livery stage from that depicted in *Plate 156* was to write 'BRITISH RAILWAYS' in full across the locomotive tankside as shown in this picture of No. 41706. Dating from 1880, when it was built as Midland Railway No. 1416, this engine was to remain in service until 1957.
Authors' Collection

Plate 160. We illustrated this engine in 1936 block style livery at *Plate 155* where its history was recorded. Here we show it when running in British Railways condition. *Authors' Collection*

Fig. 20. This drawing shows the series in the later years and should be compared with the earlier condition drawing seen in Fig. 19. *K. C. Woodhead*

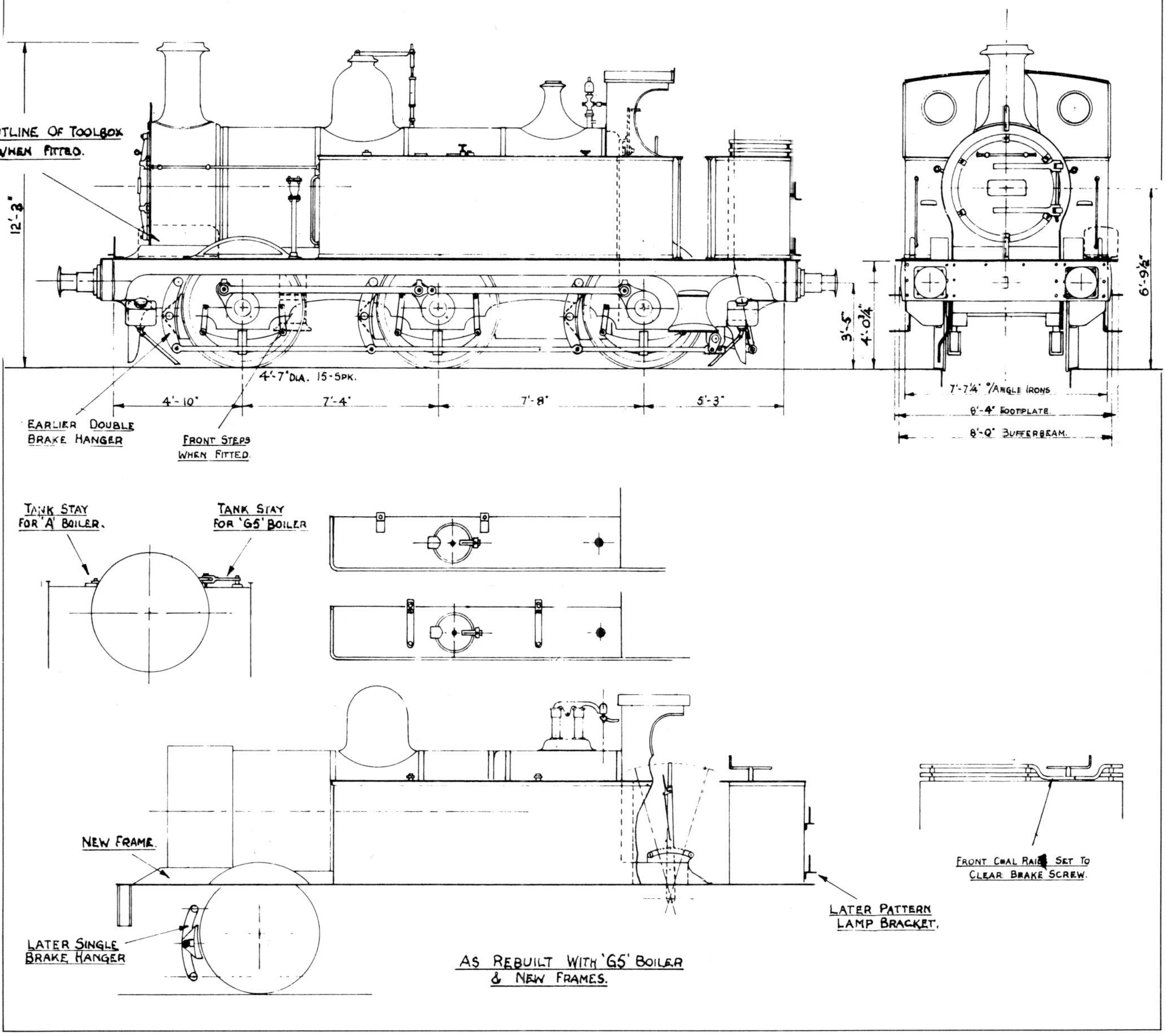

Plates 161-171. One of the authors found No. 41844 at Staveley on 9th October 1964 – and took a few pictures. We illustrated old No. 2012 at *Plate 239* in Volume 1 where its history is recorded.

R. J. Essery

1F
41844

1F
41844

1F
41844

1552 CLASS

Two orders raised for locomotives built in 1882 and 1891 formed a group of twenty, whose original Midland Railway numbers were 1552-1561 (1882) and 1982-1991 (1891). In 1907 they were renumbered 1710-1719 and 1805-1814. The basic difference between the '1377' class and '1552' class was in the height of the boiler fittings and cab. Whereas the '1377' class were to normal dimensions, those of the '1552' class were cut down, and, as far as we know, none ever received enclosed cabs. For example, the chimney heights were 11 ft. 5½ in. compared with the nominal 12 ft. 5 in. and of course the steam dome was reduced in height with the Salter valves mounted to the side of the dome instead of 'in line' (see *Plates 173/174*).

Over the years these locomotives gradually assumed a more normal configuration, firstly with taller chimneys and in due course with the conventional form of dome. However, whereas taller chimneys were in evidence at an early date, the 'cut down' domes lasted on at least one locomotive until LMS days (see *Plate 175*, engine No. 1805) and their 'reduced height' cabs seemed to stay with them to the end. Once their original domes and chimneys had both been replaced, the '1552' class engines were almost identical to the open cab locomotives of the '1377' class and are considered as such in this work.

Summary

Built at Derby 1878-1891.

Their original Midland numbers were varied (for fuller details see *Table 6*). In 1907 they were renumbered 1660-1824 (including the '1552' class variants which became Nos. 1710-1719 and 1805-1814).

Built by the Vulcan Foundry 1892.

Original Midland Railway numbers 1993-2021. In 1907 they were renumbered 1825-1844. The above series of locomotives were allocated to pages 50, 51, 52 and 53 in the 1903 Engine Diagram Book and it would seem that by 1910 only two diagrams encompassed these locomotives (see page 84).

Plate 172. 0–6–0T No. 1552 photographed c.1905, displays a locomotive in a livery other than lined crimson lake. It is not possible to be certain if it is painted black, locomotive brown, or plain crimson. Whilst there is no suggestion of black edging normally associated with locomotive brown, there is no way of being certain just what the ground colour is. No. 1552 was to become No. 1710 in 1907 and, following Nationalisation in 1948, it became No. 41710. Withdrawal was in 1957. *National Railway Museum*

Plate 173. Photographed at St. Albans in July 1902, this picture illustrates No. 1553 with the cut down dome and side-mounted safety valves but the locomotive is now fitted with a normal height Johnson cast iron chimney. Seen here in full crimson lake livery, this locomotive was to become No. 1711 in 1907 and No. 41711 following Nationalisation. Withdrawal was in 1954. *Collection Ken Nunn*

Plate 174. No. 1988 was in full crimson lake livery when photographed at Cricklewood in June 1903. It was one of a series which became Nos. 1805-1814 in 1907, built in 1891 with open cabs and cut down boiler mountings, but by the date of this picture a normal size cast iron Johnson chimney had been fitted. Becoming No. 1811 in 1907, it was withdrawn in 1954 as No. 41811. *Collection Bernard Mathews*

Plate 175. This beautiful picture of No. 1805 in LMS pre-1928 black livery clearly illustrates the cut down cab, dome and safety valves; only the chimney has been replaced – by one of Deeley's design. In due course No. 1805 entered British Railways service and was withdrawn in 1956 as No. 41805. *Collection Bernard Mathews*

Plate 176. No. 1807, with its cut-down cab, but now with normal boiler mountings, is seen in this picture displaying LMS post-1928 black livery when photographed at Derby in June 1928. Originally No. 1984, No. 1807 was withdrawn in 1938. *Authors' Collection*

Plate 177. No. 1814 displays the interesting combination of a Johnson smokebox door fitted with dogs more normally associated with the Deeley design of door. Built in 1891 as No. 1991 with cut down boiler mountings, this picture, taken c.1908, shows that a Deeley replacement chimney of normal size has been fitted. There is no evidence of lining and it is possible that this locomotive is in plain black. *National Railway Museum*

Plate 178. No. 1810 was photographed in August 1939 and this picture has been included to show the cab and bunker detail of this class. Note the extra rear 'coal rail' to increase coal capacity. The tarpaulin sheet has been rolled up and is across the cab roof. Built as No. 1987 and receiving a Belpaire boiler in 1928, this locomotive was withdrawn from service in 1947. *A. E. West*

Plate 179. No. 41712 at Kirkby in August 1964. By now a Belpaire boiler has been fitted and this old Johnson locomotive has the 'overhead wire' warning sign on the tank front. Originally No. 1554, this locomotive was withdrawn in September 1964.
Authors' Collection

TYPICAL DIAGRAM

GOODS TANK ENGINES

Nos 1600–1899

ED 1/104

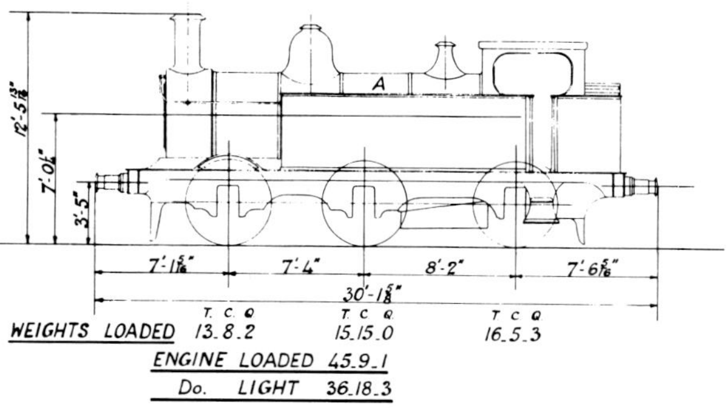

ENGINE Nos	CYLRS	BLR PRESS.	DRG WHEELS	TRACT'VE POWER
1601–1603	15"x22"	140 Lbs □"	4'-3" DIA.	10870 Lbs = 4·85 Tons
1600:1604:1606–1608 1610–1619:	17"x24"	140 Lbs □"	4'-3" DIA.	15232 Lbs = 6·80 Tons
1620–1859	17"x24"	140 Lbs □"	4'-7" DIA.	14124 Lbs = 6·30 Tons
1860–1899	17"x24"	150 Lbs □"	4'-7" DIA.	15133 Lbs = 6·75 Tons

MIDLAND RAILWAY

LOCOMOTIVE DRAWING OFFICE

DERBY

Fig. 21. ED 1/104 is a good example of a misleading diagram. Although apparently covering Nos. 1600-1899, in fact it refers only to the final series of 0–6–0Ts which became, in 1907, Nos. 1845-1899. In this respect it is identical to the 1910 Midland Railway Diagram ED 104 except that this diagram gives 42 cwts as the coal capacity and 800 gallons as the tank capacity. Nevertheless, this 1919 diagram is useful insofar as it confirms the various details of all the Class 1 0–6–0Ts as at the end of 1919. However, ED 103, which has not been reproduced, also refers to the series 1845-1899 and is almost identical except for a small variation in engine weight and the fact that it shows a cab roof ventilator. The clear message is to treat all engine diagrams with caution! *Authors' Collection*

1121 CLASS

From the start of the '1121' class, new construction of what were all later to be referred to as Class 1 0–6–0Ts incorporated a 6 in. longer wheelbase, and 3 in. higher boiler centreline. This was to accommodate A1 boilers which were 4 in. deeper in the firebox. Their cylinder size remained the same as the '1377' class but water capacity was increased by sixty gallons. Furthermore, these new engines were all built with enclosed cabs.

The construction was divided between Derby (Order No. 1395), Sharps and Stephenson (Class Q), but the interesting point is that five locomotives built by Sharps had a most curious cab arrangement; the rear spectacle plate did not exist. In fact it was a kind of open back yet enclosed design, similar to No. 1644 (*Plate 127*). See also *Plates 180/181*. Very few pictures exist which show this style of cab and it is understood that this series of five locomotives, when built, worked in the London area. Rear spectacle plates were fitted later, but we cannot be sure when and more information would be welcomed.

The Midland Railway in 1903 considered *all* of the '1121' class to be the same and we treat them as such in this volume. In later years, the entire series of Johnson 0–6–0Ts so far considered (of which engine Nos. 1845-1899 were but a part) became in 1907 Nos. 1620-1899, and were henceforward regarded as a broadly homogenous group, at least for power capacity purposes, all being classified as 1, later 1F. *Table 6* gives their 1903 dimensions and Midland classification details.

Finally, as previously mentioned, a number of locomotives within the number series 1660-1899 received Belpaire boilers and, when this was done, new front spectacle plates were necessary in order that the spectacles could be repositioned to clear the shoulders of the Belpaire firebox.

Summary

Built at Derby 1895.
The original Midland Railway numbers were 1121-1130. In 1907 the Midland Railway renumbered them 1845-1854. They were built with enclosed cabs and Nos. 1126-1130 were built with vacuum train pipes.

Built by Sharp Stewart in 1895.
Their original Midland Railway numbers were 2248-2252.
The Midland Railway renumbered them in 1907, becoming Nos. 1855-1859.
They were built with cabs having no rear spectacle plate.

Built by Robert Stephenson & Co. 1899-1900.
Their original Midland Railway numbers were 2361-2390, 2571-2580.
The Midland Railway 1907 numbers were 1860-1899.
They were all built with enclosed cabs. Many locomotives in this series received G5 Belpaire boilers during the LMS and British Railways period of ownership.
A number lasted long enough to be renumbered by British Railways by the addition of 40000 to their 1907 Midland Railway number which was also their LMS number.
The class became extinct in 1963.

Plate 180. In this view we feature the first of three pictures of No. 2250 which between them track its lifetime. Here we see it in its 'as built' condition in full crimson lake lined livery clearly displaying the curious open back cab arrangement that the five Sharp Stewart-built engines had. Readers are referred to *Plates 187 & 189* for views of the locomotive in LMS and British Railways ownership.
National Railway Museum

Plate 181. This less than perfect picture of No. 2248 illustrates a tank engine version of the 'London style' of painting (see also Volume 1, page 144). Notwithstanding other interpretations which have appeared in print, we believe that the sequence of lining on the tank sides of this crimson lake locomotive were, from the tank edge, black edging, yellow line, crimson lake, yellow lining, crimson lake. Note the elaborate manner in which the corner and front of the side tanks have been treated. No. 2248 was one of a small batch built by Sharp Stewart (2248-2252) which, for some curious reason, originally had a semi-open back cab which was later filled in with a full rear spectacle plate. We are unable to say why they were so built but it appears they did not remain as such overlong; more definite information would be welcomed from interested readers. No. 2248 was to become No. 1855 in 1907 and in its later guise was to be similar to No. 41857 seen in *Plate 189*. As British Railways No. 41855, it was to last until 1960 (see *Plate 191*). *National Railway Museum*

Plate 182. This delightful view of old No. 1129 now running as No. 1853, shows an example of a tank engine renumbered into the 1907 series but still using brass numerals. Built in 1895, this locomotive was to last until 1954 when it was withdrawn as No. 41853. Note the addition of the leading footsteps fitted from c.1903 onwards. This tank engine is in lined crimson lake and the lining on the cabside panels is interesting, being two separate panels with the black edging running the full length of the cabside beneath the cab roof. Finally it should be noted that there does not appear to be any lining on the footsteps. *National Railway Museum*

Plate 183. No. 2386 is seen here in unlined livery. Whether the base colour is crimson lake or locomotive brown is difficult to say; indeed, there is no way of knowing. The date of this picture is between 1903 and 1907, so there is always the possibility that it could be black – some goods engines were painted black as early as 1906 but their numbers were never recorded by the contemporary observers. It should also be noted that there is no evidence of the initials 'MR' on the tank side. No. 2386 was built in 1899 and was to become No. 1885 in 1907 and No. 41885 following Nationalisation. Note the absence of leading footsteps. They were fitted from an early date as the picture of No. 1853 (*Plate 182*) shows. *National Railway Museum*

Plate 184. No. 1896 in Midland Railway plain black livery. Originally No. 2577, this locomotive remained in service until the end of 1932. Note the addition of the toolbox by this date, a feature which was to continue. *Authors' Collection*

Plate 185. No. 1869 in the first LMS livery style of 1923 for freight locomotives. Note the 'LMS' on the bunker. This was to be replaced by a transferred panel which can be seen in *Plate 175.* Built as No. 2370, this locomotive was to receive a Belpaire G5 boiler in 1946 and was withdrawn in 1953 as No. 41869. *Collection Bernard Mathews*

Plate 186. No. 1865 displays the LMS post-1928 plain black freight livery with 10in gold letters. Built as No. 2366, this locomotive was to remain in service until withdrawal in 1955 as British Railways No. 41865. *Collection Bernard Mathews*

Plate 187. No. 1857 (old No. 2250 of 1895. See *Plate 180*) in Sheffield Grimesthorpe shed in September 1935. This near head-on view illustrates typical later period 'front end' changes. In its final years, as British Railways No. 41857 (see *Plate 189*), it received a Belpaire boiler before being withdrawn in 1959. *Collection Bernard Mathews*

Plate 188. This rear view of No. 1871 has been included to illustrate this particular aspect of old No. 2372. It was taken some time between 1928 and 1946 when the locomotive was withdrawn. Note the rivet work on the rear bunker, battered cab roof, lack of the centre top lamp iron and 740 gallon water capacity plate. According to the 1903 Diagram records, it should have read 800 gallons. *Authors' Collection*

Plate 189. In this view we see another example of one of the five locomotives built by Sharp Stewart in 1895 (see also *Plates 180/187*). Originally No. 2250, No. 41857 is seen here in early British Railways livery. Note that the original cab with its narrower sidesheets has been retained. *A. G. Ellis*

Plate 190. A Derby-built engine, No. 41853 started life in 1895 as Midland Railway No. 1129. In this picture c.1948 we see it in the first style of British Railways livery. *Authors' Collection*

Plate No. 191. Old No. 2248 is seen here as British Railways No. 41855. Readers are referred to *Plate 181* for an 'as built' view of this engine and its history. *A. G. Ellis*

Plate 192. No. 2444 became No. 1903 in 1907 and was rebuilt with a Belpaire G5½ boiler in 1930. The LMS 1934 renumbering scheme saw a change to No. 7203, and withdrawal as British Rail No. 47203 was in 1960. At the time of this photograph, which was taken some time between construction in 1899 and renumbering in 1907, the locomotive was running in fully lined crimson lake livery.

Authors' Collection

2441 CLASS

The final design of six-coupled side tank engines to be built by the Midland Railway was a series of sixty much larger locomotives constructed during a four year period and allocated to two separate class letters, 'S' and 'U', the latter being divided into 'U' and 'U2' as indicated in *Table 6*. It is difficult to understand why this series was allocated three different class numbers, but the 1903 Diagram Book confirms that they were. We shall regard them as one class only.

Summary

Built by the Vulcan Foundry 1899-1902.

Their original Midland Railway numbers were 2441-2460 and 2741-2780.

The Midland Railway renumbered them in 1907 and they became Nos. 1900-1959.

They were renumbered 7200-7259 by the LMS under their 1934 renumbering scheme and at nationalisation 40000 was added to those numbers.

All were built with enclosed cabs and many were built with condensing apparatus. All were rebuilt with G5½ Belpaire boilers between 1919-1942.

The class became extinct in 1966.

In 1910 the condenser-fitted locomotives were allocated to Engine Diagram 105 and the non-condenser locomotives to Engine Diagram 106.

In 1919 locomotive No. 1934 was rebuilt with a G5½ Belpaire boiler and in this condition it was allocated to ED106A. It was not until 1942 that the last locomotive was rebuilt in this form (No. 7259, ex-Nos. 2780/1959, see *Plate 209*).

It is worthwhile noting that this series of locomotives, in their rebuilt Belpaire boiler condition, provided the basis for the design of the LMS standard shunting tank locomotives known as Standard Class 3 (later 3F), 481 of which were constructed by the LMS. The Midland engines were to last as long as the standard LMS locomotives and were to remain in service almost to the end of steam on British Railways. None were preserved.

Front footsteps began to be fitted in 1903 but a photograph of No. 2758 taken c.1905 shows the engine still without. An interesting feature on this class concerned the front corner of the side tank. Those locomotives fitted with condensers had a squared corner with 'cooling slots' (see *Plates 218-221*). Because the tank sides would get hot and thereby cause the paint to blister, an outer panel was provided with an airspace between this panel and the tank side proper. This arrangement produced a squared corner as opposed to the rounded corner of the non-fitted locomotives, a feature clearly seen in the various plates.

Whilst the condenser-fitted locomotives worked in the London area, a number of non-condenser engines went to Bromsgrove as bankers on the Lickey Incline and as such were to be found on this work for many years. They were by far the Midland Railway's most powerful shunting tank engines and it is interesting to note their 1920 allocation which was: Cricklewood 29, Kentish Town 12, Worcester 8 (Lickey Incline), South Wales 8 (shared between Brecon and Upper Bank), with one at Buxton and two at Bradford.

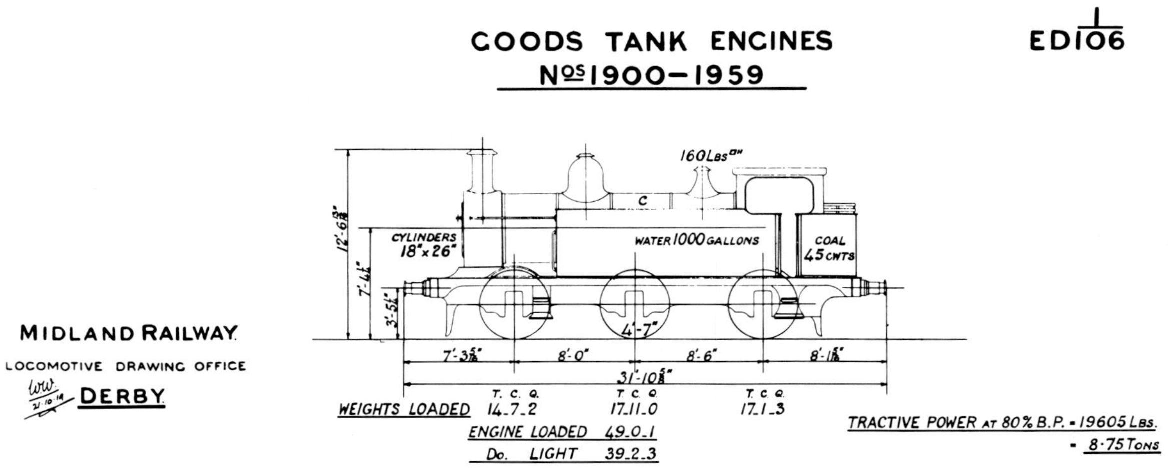

Fig. 22. ED 1/106 was the Midland Railway's 1910 diagram for the non-condenser equipped locomotives of this class.
Authors' Collection

Plate 193. This picture shows condenser-fitted locomotive No. 2443. The engine is in a highly decorated crimson lake style with guard irons, footsteps and sandboxes lined out. In addition, there is lining on the main frame at the base of the smokebox, on the ends of the buffer planks, and the cab sides and spectacle plate have been fully treated; even the wheel centres have a central circle with black axle ends. No. 2443 became No. 1902 in 1907 and No. 7202 as part of the 1934 LMS renumbering programme before being withdrawn as British Railways No. 47202 in 1966. A rebuild in 1926 saw the fitting of a Belpaire boiler. *National Railway Museum*

Plate 194. No. 2761 at Trafford Park. This locomotive was to become No. 1940 and was fitted with a G5½ boiler in 1925. It became No. 7240 c.1934 and, following Nationalisation, was renumbered again, becoming No. 47240. Withdrawal was in 1957. The locomotive is in full crimson lake livery with lining around the base of the dome, lining on the framing at the base of the smokebox, bottom of the valance, guard irons, sandboxes, brake hangers and footsteps supports. The axle centres of the wheels are black with a fine yellow line and the bottom edge of the frames were also fine yellow lined, edged black – in all a good example of the full crimson lake livery as applied to a member of this class. *Collection Roger Carpenter*

Plate 195. We have used this picture of 2741, a condenser-fitted engine, to offer a comparison with the non-condenser locomotive seen in *Plate 194.* Built in 1901, No. 2741 was to become first 1920, then No. 7220 before being withdrawn in 1956 as British Railways No. 47220. *Authors' Collection*

Fig. 23. We show here the General Arrangement drawing for the 'S' class condensing tank engines. Note that the drawing shows curved front corners to the side tanks. Later this was to be altered (see caption to Plate 206, engine No. 7224, and captions to Plates 218 & 219).

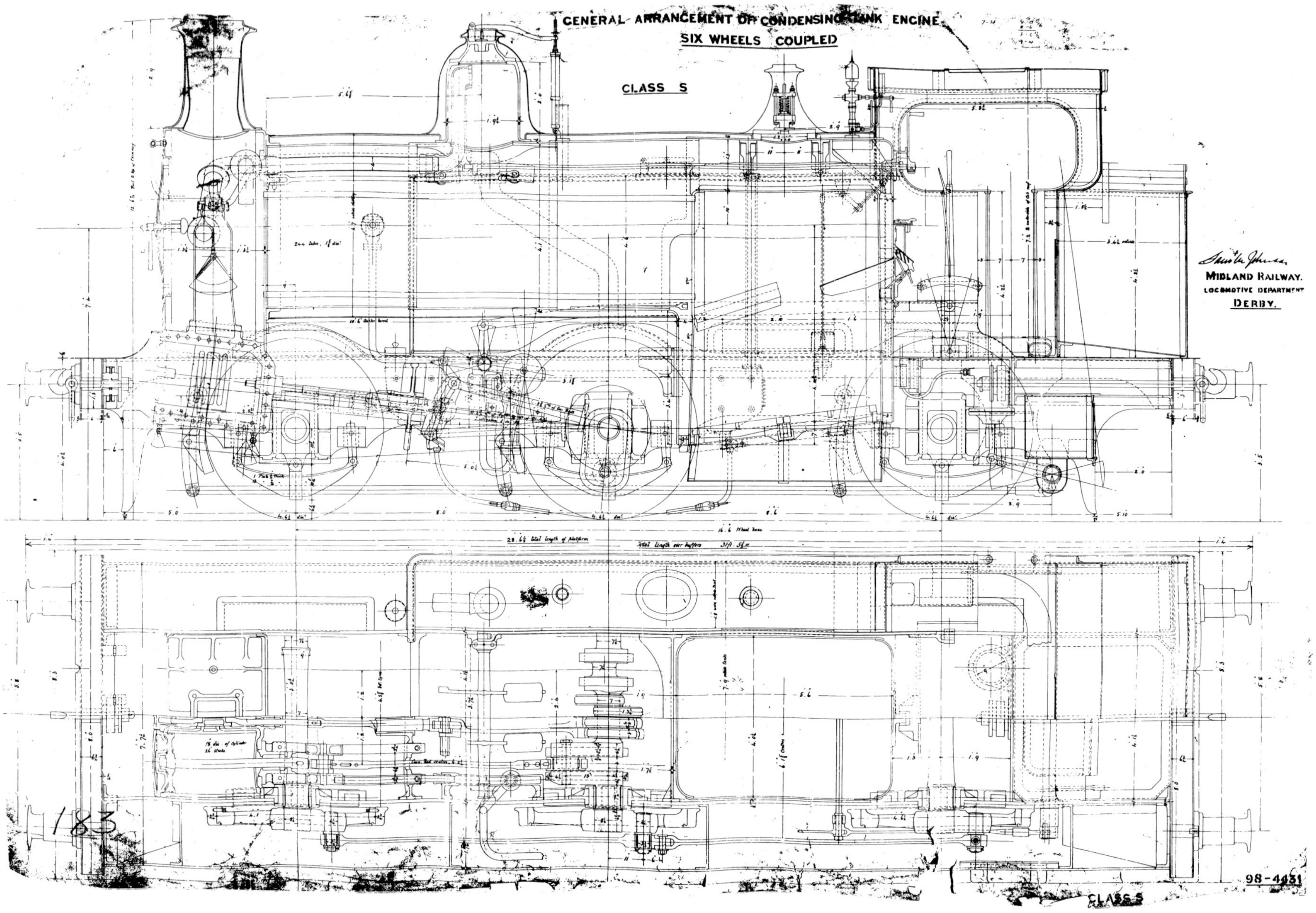

Plate 196. This interesting view of No. 1941, originally No. 2762, illustrates the use of brass numbers on a tank locomotive following the 1907 renumbering scheme. It was c.1909 before the use of the large transfer numbers were to be seen on tank engines. Other examples are to be seen in Volume 4. Whereas these views show black engines, No. 1941 carries the simplified crimson lake livery. There is no 'below the footplate' lining other than on the wheels adjacent to the tyres, and the boiler lagging bands are unlined except the leading one next to the smokebox. Note, too, that whereas locomotives without leading footsteps did not have a handrail on the tank ends, once a footstep had been fitted, this feature appeared. In 1925 a Belpaire boiler was fitted and later No. 1941 became LMS No. 7241 (BR 47241) before being withdrawn from service in 1960. *National Railway Museum*

Plate 197. Old No. 2773, built in 1902, is seen here in lined crimson lake livery carrying its 1907 number. *National Railway Museum*

Plate 198. Taken at Bromsgrove, this picture illustrates No. 1947 in plain black livery. A number of this class were employed upon banking duties on the Lickey Incline, including this one. Originally No. 2768, this locomotive was to be equipped with a Belpaire boiler in 1925 and following renumbering c.1934 (No. 7247) it was again renumbered by British Railways and withdrawn as No. 47247 in 1959. *W. L. Good*

Plate 199. No. 1943 in late Midland days at Kentish Town when in plain black livery. Note the Furness lubricator at the base of the smokebox, later to be removed. No. 1943 was originally No. 2764 and in 1934 it was renumbered 7243. By now it was fitted with a G5½ boiler, this change dating from 1926. The 1948 renumbering by British Railways added 40,000 to its LMS number, and withdrawal as No. 47243 was in 1957.
Authors' Collection

Plate 200. No. 1925 is a condenser-fitted locomotive, originally No. 2746, built in 1901. Reboilering was in 1926 and in 1934 it was renumbered 7225. British Railways ownership saw it become No. 47225 and withdrawal was in 1963. The locomotive displays a flat smokebox door with a vertical handle but no horizontal handrail. Note that there are two upper lamp irons, one on the top of the smokebox, the other on the smokebox door. Photographed at Clapham Junction in April 1920.
Authors' Collection

Plate 201. No. 1959 had the distinction of being the last locomotive of this class to be reboilered with a G5½ boiler – conversion took place in 1942 when numbered 7259. This picture shows the locomotive (originally No. 2780 built in 1902) in plain black livery at Derby in 1922. Withdrawal as No. 47259 was in 1962.

Collection Ken Nunn

Plate 202. Built as No. 2742, this locomotive became No. 1921 in 1907. In 1934 it became LMS 7221 and a Belpaire boiler was not fitted until 1940. Withdrawal as British Railways No. 47221 was in 1961.

Collection Bernard Mathews

Plate 203. No. 1953 in LMS ownership. Photographed at Stoke in May 1932, this view illustrates the LMS post-1928 black freight livery. Note that the Furness lubricator, previously at the base of the smokebox, has been removed. Originally No. 2774, it was built in 1902 and was not fitted with a G5½ Belpaire boiler until 1940. Withdrawal as BR No. 47253 was in 1955. *W. L. Good*

GOODS TANK ENGINES
BETN NOS 1900 & 1959
G5½ REBUILDS

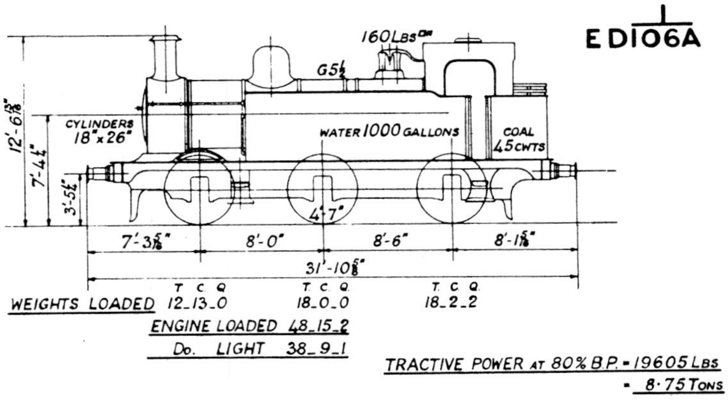

Fig. 24. ED 1/106A. This 1920 Midland Railway diagram was issued following the rebuilding of No. 1934 and applied to those members of the class which had been rebuilt with G5½ Belpaire boilers. Note the more modern appearance which the rounded eaves cab gave to the rebuilds, when compared to their original condition. It was the cab rather than the Belpaire boiler which provided the principal visual change. *Authors' Collection*

Plate 204. In this view we see No. 1930 at Bromsgrove in February 1920 following rebuilding with a Belpaire boiler. Later to become 7230, then 47230, service continued until withdrawal by British Railways in 1964. *W. L. Good*

Plate 205. No. 1951 at Kentish Town in LMS pre-1928 freight livery. Built as No. 2772, this locomotive was reboilered in 1923 and lasted until 1958 when it was withdrawn as British Railways No. 47251. Note the lamp irons on the smokebox door in addition to the one at the base of the chimney. *Collection Bernard Mathews*

Plate 206. No. 7224 at Cricklewood in June 1937. Note the smokebox door lamp iron and absence of a lamp iron on the top of the smokebox. The lever running from the rear of the tank to the base of the smokebox is the control apparatus to divert the exhaust steam into the side tanks rather than up the chimney. Note the 'square end' to the tank side of the condenser locomotives where an additional sheet was attached to the sides and front to provide an 'air space' between the actual tank side and the visible tank side. The water in the tanks could become very hot indeed and cause blistering of the tank sides, hence the need to have a false side to preserve the exterior paintwork. Condenser-fitted locomotives are distinguished by this detail and, from a modeller's point of view, the tank sides are wider. Finally, although not very visible, there is a gap at the end of the tank (see *Plates 218-221*). No. 7224 was originally No. 2745 built in 1901 and was reboilered with a G5½ boiler in 1923. The 1907 MR renumbering saw the locomotive become No. 1924 and under British Railways it became No. 47224. It was withdrawn in 1962. *Collection A. G. Ellis*

Plate 207. No. 7232 was photographed at Derby in May 1935. Built as No. 2753 in 1902, it became No. 1932 in 1907 and No. 7232 under the LMS 1934 renumbering scheme. Reboilering was in 1925 and withdrawal as British Railways No. 47232 was in 1955. The locomotive is in plain black livery with gold insignia. Actually, they are black-shaded gold transfers which, of course, show up as plain gold on a black locomotive. *Collection V. Forster*

Plate 208. No. 1914 as reboilered and condenser fitted. Built in 1900 as No. 2455, it was fitted with a G5½ boiler in 1927 and became No. 7214 c.1934. Withdrawal was in 1959 as British Railways No. 47214. *Photomatic*

Plates 209-221. We conclude with a series of pictures illustrating these engines in their final years and on this page we show three pictures of Nos. 47259 (*Plate 209*), 47220 (*Plate 210*) and 47216 (*Plate 211*). *Plate 209* depicts the last engine to be rebuilt but with the first style of British Railways livery written in full across the tank side. An earlier view of the engine, together with its history, is at *Plate 201*. *Plates 210 & 211* illustrate condenser engines No. 47220 and No. 47216, the latter at Cricklewood in August 1956. Both locomotives carry the final style of British Railways livery. *A. G. Ellis and Authors' Collection*

Plates 212 to 217. The first four views show No. 47202 in 1964 and have been included to give readers the opportunity of seeing in close-up some details of a condenser-fitted locomotive. *Plate 213* shows the left-hand side with the control lever visible. *Plate 214* is the right-hand view and, like the left-hand side, the 'clacks' can be seen. This side also shows the ejector used to create the vacuum and to release the brakes of a fitted train. As mentioned in Volume 1, Midland locomotives were themselves braked by steam. *Plate 215* shows the front end, note the lamp irons designed to take London area destination boards. The 'air space' mentioned in *Plate 218* can be seen in each of these views. *Plates 216 & 217* show a bunker rear view of 'non condenser' locomotives Nos. 47257 and 47201 showing the extension plate attached to the coal rails. These were fitted from the mid-1930s to reduce coal spillage following the introduction of mechanical coaling plants. Note also the extra rainstrip fitted to the cab roof by the LMS (compare No. 1934, *Plate 118*) and also the protective cover over the top of the end train pipe, this also dating from the mechanical coaling era. *Authors' Collection*

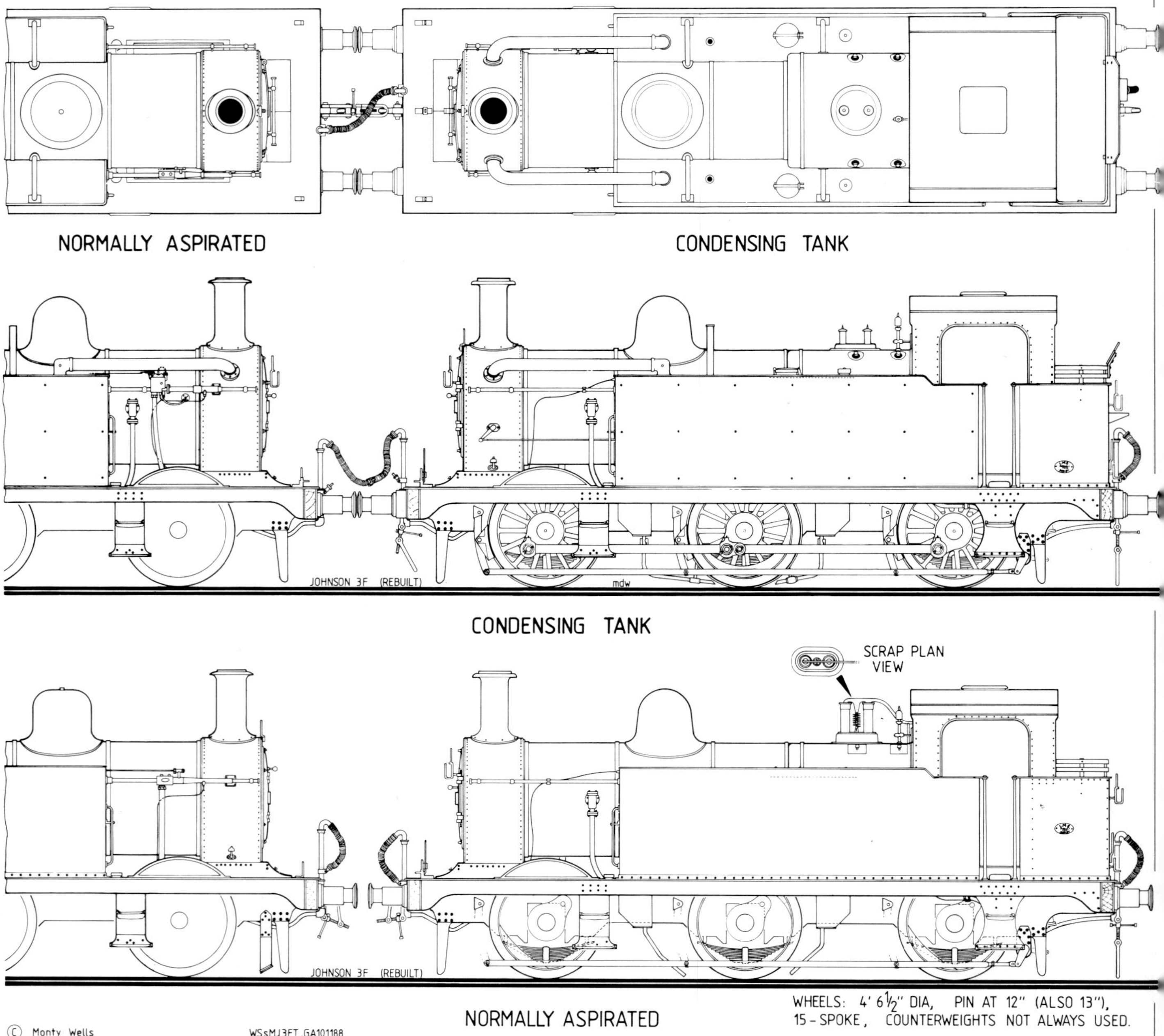

WSsMJ3FT.GA101188

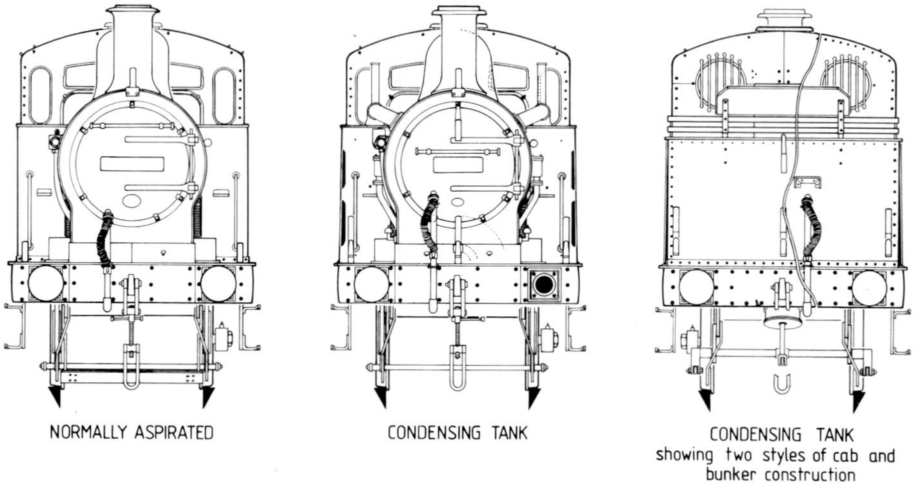

Fig. 25. This drawing illustrates the class following rebuilding with a Belpaire boiler and with a rounded eaves cab.

Drawn by Monty Wells

Some detail drawn from photographs. Views show greatest possible mixture of detail, not any one engine, so views do not necessarily relate.

Plates 218 to 221. Four front close-up pictures of No. 47201 have been included to give readers detailed views of a 'non condenser' locomotive except, of course, this locomotive was originally so fitted, see slots at the tank corner. *Plates 218-20* show the right- and left-hand views of the tanks, clack valves, large ejector and footsteps. *Plate 221* shows the left-hand side of the cab; note the broken part of the footstep support. The turned up corner to the footsteps was a later LMS safety modification applied to all locomotives of Midland origin.
Authors' Collection

TABLE 6 – JOHNSON 0-6-0T CLASSES
CLASS 1 & 3 ENGINES

								BOILER						FIREBOX			WHEELS		ENGINE WEIGHT				
1903 Diagram Page No.	*Order No. or Class*	*Built by*	*Quantity Built*	*Date of Building*	*Pre 1907 Numbers*	*1907 Renumbering*	*Cylinders*	*Centre Line*	*Diameter*	*Length*	*Tubes*	*Diameter*	*Working Pressure*	*Length*	*Grate Area in Sq Ft*	*Total Heating Surface in Sq Ft*	*Driving*	*Tyres*	*Empty*	*Loaded*	*Water Capacity in Gallons*	*Coal Capacity*	*REMARKS*
65	A	Neilsons	18	1874/5	1102-1115 1127-1130	1620-1633 1645-1648	17″ × 24″	6′9″	4′2″	10′0″	213	1¾″	140 PSI	5′0″	14.5	1115	4′6½″	2¾″	35.11.2	42.9.3	900	24 cwt	1102 class. These locomotives were given a separate diagram number when they went onto the duplicate list. Carried earlier style of Johnson domes and safety valve trumpet. All in green livery when built.
54	A	Neilsons	11	1875	1116-1120 2253-2258	1634-1638 1639-1644																	
	A	Vulcan	11	1875/6	1131-1141	1645-1659																	
53	204	Derby	10	1878	1377-1388	1660-1669	17″ × 24″	6′9″	4′2″	10′0″	213	1¾″	140 PSI	5′0″	14.5	1115	4′6½″	2¾″	34.18.0	42.11.2	740	42 cwt	1377 class. Engines built before 1882 fitted with 4′ [illegible]″ driving wheels. Carried later style of Johnson boiler mountings when new. General Note: Order nos 204/218/262 green livery when new. Together with Order Nos. 239 and 340 below.
	218	Derby	20	1878/9	1347-1356 1387-1396	1680-1689 1670-1679																	
	262	Derby	10	1880	1410-1419	1700-1709																	
	496	Derby	15	1884	1090-1092 1094/5 1677-1686	1740-1744 1730-1739																	
	499	Derby	15	1884/5	1096-1100 1687-1696	1755-1759 1745-1754																	
	824	Derby	10	1889/90	200, 201, 213/4/7, 222/3, 1093, 1101, 1431	1760-1769																	
	869	Derby	10	1890	203, 1848-1852 1973-1976	1780-1785 1786-1789																	
	883	Derby	10	1890	880-889	1795-1804																	
	924	Derby	5	1890	1977-1981	1790-1794																	
53	340	Derby	10	1882	1552-1561	1710-1719	17″ × 24″	6′9″	4′2″	10′0″	213	1¾″	140 PSI	5′0″	14.5	1115	4′6½″	2¾″	34.18.0	42.11.2	740	42 cwt	1552 class. Built with cut down boiler mountings, 11′5½″ rail to chimney top.
	968		10	1891	1982-1991	1805-1814																	
51	239	Derby	10	1879	220-221 1420-1427	1690-1699	17″ × 24″	6′9″	4′2″	10′0″	213	1¾″	140 PSI	5′0″	14.5	1115	4′6½″	2¾″	34.18.0	42.11.2	740	42 cwt	1377 class. It is far from clear why this series was not allocated to page 53. 1725-1729 (1907 nos built with enclosed cabs).
	414	Derby	10	1883	210-212, 215/6 218/9, 1397-1399	1720-1729																	
	854	Derby	10	1890	1102-1106 1843-1847	1770-1779																	
	991	Derby	10	1891	1992, 1107-1115	1815-1824																	
50	N	Vulcan	20	1892	1993-2012	1825-1844	17″ × 24″	6′9¼″	4′2″	10′0″	213	1¾″	140 PSI	5′0″	14.5	1115	4′6½″	2¾″	34.18.0	42.11.2	740	42 cwt	1377 class. It would seem that ¼″ boiler centre line was sufficient to warrant a fresh page in the diagram book.
49	Q	Sharps	5	1895	2248-2252	1855-1859	17″ × 24″	7′0″	4′2″	10′0″	213	1¾″	140/150 PSI	5′0″	14.5	1120	4′6½″	2¾″	35.4.3 37.2.2	43.16.2 45.14.0	800	42 cwt	1121 class. Note alternate weights. A1 boiler with additional 5 sq feet heating surface in firebox. Diagram quotes rail to chimney 12′6$\frac{1}{16}$″ for contractor-built and 12′6$\frac{9}{16}$″ for Derby-built locomotives. Sharps engines built for East London lines.
		Stephensons	30	1899	2361-2390	1860-1889																	
		Stephensons	10	1899/90	2571-2580	1890-1899																	
	1395	Derby	10	1895	1121-1130	1845-1854																	
48	S	Vulcan	20	1899/90	2441-2460	1900-1919	18″ × 26″	7′4″	4′2″	10′6″	244	1⅝″	160 PSI	5′6″	16.0	1252	4′6½″	2¾″	40.2.1	48.16.3	1000	45 cwt	2441 class.
			10	1901	2741-2750	1920-1929																	
47	U	Vulcan	10	1902	2751-2760	1930-1939	18″ × 26″	7′4⅛″	4′2″	10′6″	244	1⅝″	160 PSI	5′6″	16.0	1252	4′6¾″	2⅞″	39.2.0	48.9.1	1000	45 cwt	
	U2	Vulcan	20	1902	2761-2780	1940-1959																	

Source: Generally the 1903 engine diagram book

ANNUAL AVERAGES – MIDLAND COMPARED TO ALL U.K. RAILWAYS

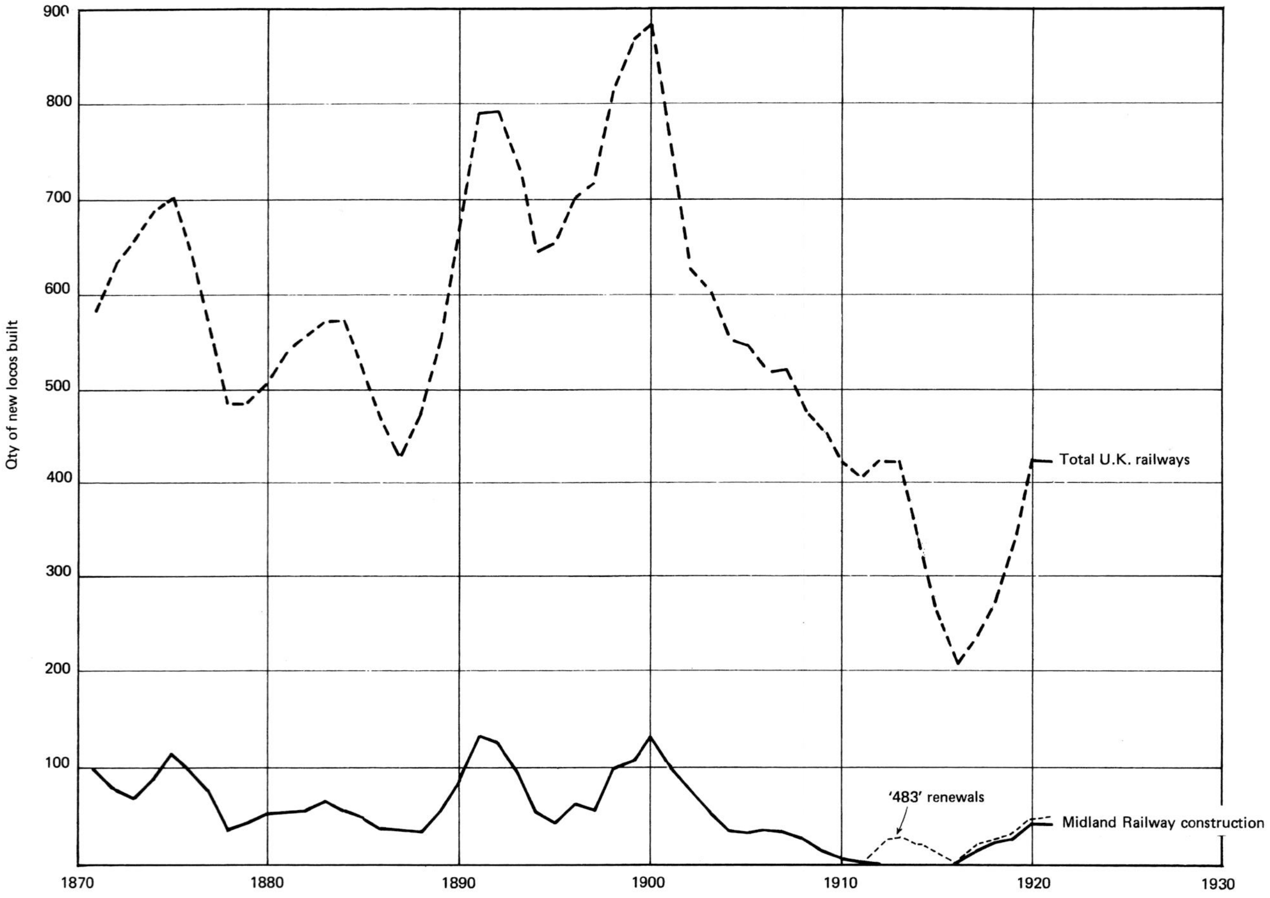

MIDLAND RAILWAY TRAIN MILES

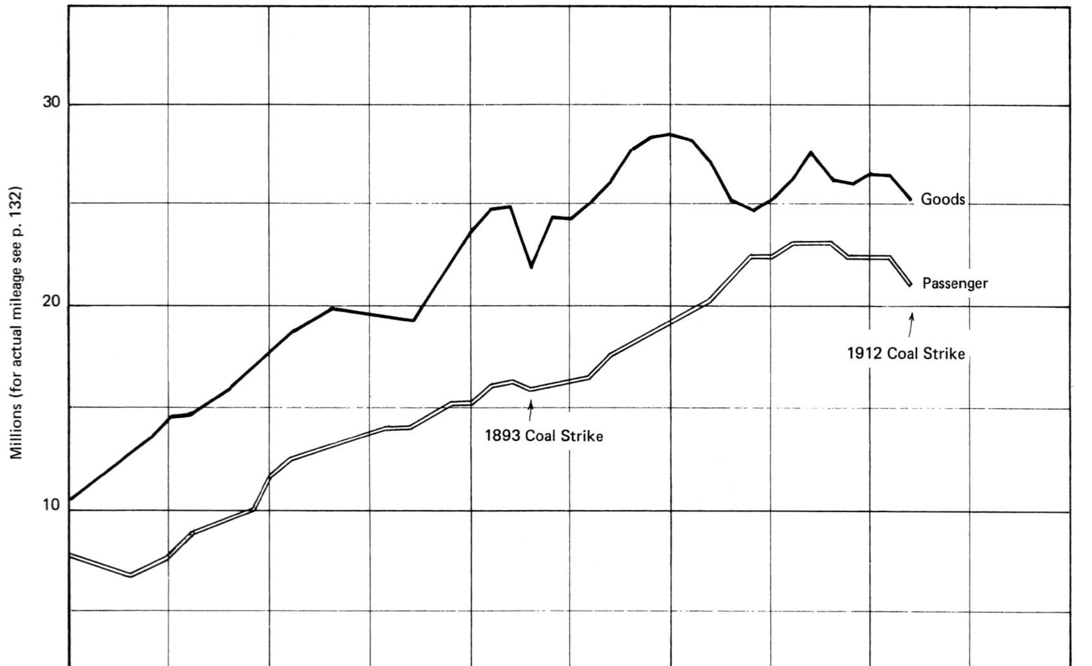

CHAPTER SIX

LOCOMOTIVE BUILDING ON THE MIDLAND RAILWAY 1870-1922

An analysis based on research notes provided by C. P. Atkins, Librarian, National Railway Museum

Authors' Note

Although we have added a few linking comments to the data provided by Philip Atkins – generally to relate his remarks to our own observations both in this and other volumes – it would be wrong for us to claim more than a peripheral contribution to the facts and figures quoted in this chapter, or for the tabulations and diagrams prepared to go with them, not all of which were reproduced due to lack of space. Once again we repeat our thanks for Mr. Atkins' generosity in permitting us to use this information, some of which, in fact, forms part of his more extended research into the linkage between the work of the Derby and Ashford (SE & CR) drawing offices via the person of James Clayton.

Although this chapter is mainly concerned with analysing the locomotive building policy of the Midland Railway as revealed by surviving statistics, including a modest attempt to relate them to some of the outside factors which may have affected the issue, it also includes some new observations on MR locomotive design policy which should serve to complement our own comments, particularly in Volume 2 of this series.

RJE/DJ

LOCOMOTIVE BUILDING 1870-1922

In terms of total locomotive stock, the Midland Railway ranked third only after the London & North Western and Great Western Railways. The locomotive policy of the MR differed considerably from that of the LNWR and GWR, not least being the heavy dependence upon the private locomotive industry for locomotive supply; the other two concerns were, to all intents and purposes, self-sufficient. Despite the plethora of published literature concerning the British steam locomotive, no year by year analysis of construction, and its possible relation to determining factors, appears to have been made for any railway, major or minor. This analysis attempts to make the effort for the bulk of the locomotives covered in this series of volumes.

New locomotive construction can be said to be made up of two main components – simple 'one-to-one' replacement of life-expired locomotives, plus additional locomotives to cover increasing traffic on the established network and for additional traffic due to the opening of new lines. In the latter respect the last *major* development on the MR was the completion and opening of the Carlisle extension in 1876. Interestingly, this event was not reflected in a sharp increase in train mileage as tabulated in the Board of Trade Annual Railway Returns. Total train mileage on the MR increased by one million per annum *on average* between 1870 and 1900. The two components, passenger and freight mileage, did not always increase in unison, thus freight mileage between 1884 and 1887 fell back on the 1883 figure before increasing once more, with *total* mileage actually levelling out in the mid-1880s; a sharp reversal occurred in 1893 as a result of the severe coal strike during the latter half of that year.

Four years later, industry was enjoying an unprecedented boom, but from July 1897 to January 1898 the engineering branch suffered from a strike which hit several of the major locomotive builders. Delivery of locomotives ordered by the Midland during the winter of 1897-8 was delayed from the customary 6-9 months to 18-24 months, with none at all delivered in 1898, during which total train mileage increased by two million the exceptional step of ordering no fewer than forty 2–6–0s from the United States was taken in early 1899. These were all delivered before the end of the same year, which witnessed exceptionally intense general industrial activity, and ended with the outbreak of the (2nd) South African War.

During 1899 the Midland Railway put into traffic no fewer than 179 new locomotives, and 172 in 1892, figures never equalled by any other British railway before 1923. Maxima for the LNWR was 131 in 1921, and only 105 by the GWR in 1872 and 1874. Between 1870 and 1900 an average of 72 new engines per annum entered traffic on the Midland, whereas Derby Works' maximum yearly potential output was about 50. Over the period 1870-1922 around four new locomotives were built 'outside' for every three constructed at Derby Works, which additionally, however, built engines from time to time for the Somerset & Dorset Joint Railway (including the celebrated 2–8–0s) and the Northern Counties Committee in Ulster.

Interestingly, and doubtless significantly, the third greatest input of new locomotives in the Midland occurred in 1876 at 148 (which included fifty 2–4–0s) only twenty of which were built at Derby. However, during 1885-1889 *all* new locomotives were exclusively built at Derby, which doubtless reflected the hiatus in traffic levels earlier referred to. Looked at over a broader period, Derby built all 95 4–2–2s and most of the 4–4–0s, but orders for 0–6–0s tended to be placed with contractors. A practical explanation is that the passenger engines were usually ordered in small batches of only ten and twenty, frequently incorporating subtle successive improvements, whereas the

0—6—0s were often ordered fifty at a time, and were basically little changed between 1874 and 1902. Probably Derby's greatest manufacturing feat was to turn out all forty Deeley 0—6—4Ts in the space of only nine months during 1907.

Just as total train mileage effectively levelled out after 1902, so did *reported* total locomotive stock which was consistently quoted at 2,790 between 1903 and 1907, and 2,800 between 1908 and 1912. From 1913 came a change in the mode of compilation of the Board of Trade Annual Returns requiring capital plus *duplicate* locomotive stock. For the Midland this was now given as 3,019, which, if one deducts the 94 engines taken over from the London Tilbury & Southend Railway in 1912 (which was still returned separately that year), gives a figure of 2,925, 125 up on 1912. Quite apart from inevitable scrappings of Kirtley locomotives, no new locomotives whatever were built by or for the Midland Railway between 1910 and 1916, with the exception of the two prototype Class 4 0—6—0s in 1911. Just how many locomotives were in MR duplicate stock at any given time prior to 1913 is not easy to determine, but 158 engines with the 'A' suffix are known to have been included in the 1907 renumbering schedule.

New locomotive construction resumed with series production of Class 4 0—6—0s in 1917, and a total of 190 were built, including fifty from Armstrong Whitworth & Co. in 1921-1922. In addition were five 0—4—0Ts, plus the Lickey 0—10—0 No. 2290. Despite the addition of 196 new locomotives to stock between 1917 and 1922, the grand total at 31st December 1922 was precisely the same as nine years earlier. In between times it had ranged only from 2,921 to 2,927.

Although (technically) no new locomotives were built between 1912 and 1916, the renewal of no fewer than 102 4—4—0s to '483' class during that period alone, requiring at the very least new boilers, cylinders, and main frames, must have represented the equivalent of say 70-80 entirely new engines. Furthermore, from 1903 many Johnson 0—6—0s were renewed with new frames and/or boilers, which also represented a form of 'new' construction. It was probably due to this massive rebuilding that the level of new locomotive input fluctuated much more widely on the Midland Railway than upon any of its contemporaries. But it also meant that statistically, disregarding the LTS contingent, the average age of its locomotive stock at 31st December 1922 was the oldest at 31 years, compared to a national average of approximately 25 years. For the LNWR (Division A) average locomotive age was 24½ years, while the newest fleet was on the Great Northern at only 19 years.

If, however, one plots 3-year averages of new locomotives to stock for the Midland Railway and the UK as a whole, one finds the former, which was indeed a component in its own right, remarkably reflects trends in the latter. Distinct peaks occur at 1875, 1892 and 1900. Thus, although it is easy to construe the Midland 1875 peak as concomitant with the need for additional motive power to work the S & C line, this might alternatively have merely reflected a contemporary national boom. The later 1880s show a distinct depression, nationally, which was when Derby Works met all the MR's needs. This was followed by a very sharp rise c.1891-2, which was abruptly dashed by the 1893 Coal Strike. The sharp rise thereafter in the latter half of the 1890s, culminating in the actual importation of loco-

NEW LOCOMOTIVE CONSTRUCTION ON THE MR, LNWR & GWR, 1870-1922

Period	*Works*	*MR Con-tractors*	*Total*	*Works*	*LNWR Con-tractors*	*Total*	*Works*	*GWR Con-tractors*	*Total*
1870-4	85	363	448	441	16[1]	467	279	0	479
1875-9	116	239	355	443	0	433	339	0	359
1880-4	188	110	298	461	0	461	271	0	271
1885-9	169	0	269	319	0	319	195	0	195
1890-4	162	345	507	556	0	556	305	0	305
1895-9	102	283	385	567	0	567	337	0	337
1900-4	132	237	369	456	0	456	375	1[3]	376
1905-9	146	0	146	435	0	435	270	2[3]	272
1910-4	2	0	2	353	0	353	239	0	239
1915-9	66	0	66	244	20[2]	264	180	0	180
1920-2	80	50	130	130	90[2]	200[5]	90	35[4]	125
Total	1248	1627	2875	4405	126	4531	3100	38	3138

1 Met-type 4—4—0Ts
2 'Prince of Wales' 4—6—0s
3 French-built compound 4—4—2s
4 63XX 2—6—0s
5 Including LNWR Division A only in 1922

Year	Total Route Mileage			Total Train Mileage (x 1,000,000)			Reported Loco Stock		
	LNWR	GWR	MR	LNWR	GWR	MR	LNWR	GWR	MR
1870	1507	1387	972	25.04	16.08	17.87	1591	929	850
1875	1604	1599	1139	31.89	20.64	22.52	2189	1223	1196
1880	1736	2148	1365	35.10	27.86	29.56	2293	1550	1465
1885	1828	2384	1399	38.22	29.86	33.57	2507	1582	1732
1890	1877	2481	1382	41.90	34.86	39.06	2600	1620	1926
1895	1908	2511	1397	41.66	38.55	40.6	2781	1750	2252
1900	1937	2627	1437	49.22	46.41	48.02	2984	1988	2615
1905	1947	2755	1482	46.67	47.53	47.92	3035	2355	2790
1910	1966	2993	1531	47.46	51.89	48.90	3053	2596	2800

motives from the USA, by several railways including the Midland in particular, was actually less from trough to peak, as it had been between 1887 and 1891.

After 1900, national demand dropped steadily, again mirrored by the Midland, showing some signs of levelling out c.1910-1913, when on the MR new locomotive construction temporarily ceased, regaining this level in 1920-1921, when there was a revival on the MR. The sharp national fall 1913-1916 can quite definitely be attributed to the somewhat artificial effects of World War I. It is conceivable that but for this, new construction at Derby could have resumed earlier; for example, the Lickey 0–10–0 was authorised in May 1914 but not completed until December 1919. It is also conceivable that series production of Class 4 0–6–0s would otherwise have also commenced c.1915, but for the lack of manpower and general resources.

The reason for the high average age of the Midland locomotive stock was simply the low level of genuine new construction after 1909. In 1910 average age had been a respectable twenty years, in 1900 nineteen years, and in 1890 eighteen years. But, had the Midland remained as an independent entity after 1922, a major restocking programme would have to have begun within a short period. In a sense this is precisely what happened under the newly formed LMS, which built large numbers of new Class 2 and Class 4 4–4–0s, Class 4 0–6–0s, and Class 3F 0–6–0Ts during the 1920s. Although many of these engines actually replaced large numbers of ex-LNWR engines which strictly speaking were not life-expired, they were probably first envisaged as overdue replacements for the more elderly elements of the Midland fleet. In the event, the latter soldiered on for even longer than perhaps the Midland itself may have intended.

Comparisons with the LNWR and GWR reveal that both these enterprises experienced a general levelling out of traffic, as measured by total train miles, after 1900. Neither of these concerns, however, showed the same low level of new locomotive construction as did the Midland. Circa 1904 the total locomotive stock of the LNWR actually declined as frantic scrapping of Webb three-cylinder compound passenger engines outpaced new construction. True to form, however, under Whale, Crewe built new classes of engine in prodigious quantities, i.e. 90 'Precursors', 105 'Experiments', and 170 19 in. 4–6–0s. On the GWR, locomotives were turned out in more measured quantities, but both dwarfed the Midland, thus:

New Locomotives to Stock 1903-1922

	LNWR	GWR	MR
1903	90	89	41
1904	66	48	36
1905	77	70	31
1906	88	97	30
1907	95	52	46
1908	92	30	26
1909	83	23	14
1910	84	43	0
1911	74	54	2
1912	71	63	0
1913	72	52	0
1914	52	27	0
1915	44	25	0
1916	57	33	0
1917	48	42	15
1918	50	48	28
1919	65	32	23
1920	50	42	35
1921	131	60	21

MR TRAFFIC AND LOCOMOTIVE STATISTICS 1870-1922

Year	*Train Mileage x 1,000,000* Pass	Frt	Total	Reported Loco Stock	Net Increase	*New Locomotives* Con-tractors	Derby Works	Total	With-drawals
1870	7.57	10.41	17.98	850	114	118	19	137	23
1871	7.35	11.31	18.66	940	90	100	8	108	18
1872	7.09	12.07	19.16	984	44	35	13	48	4
1873	6.82	12.77	19.59	1040	56	51	21	72	15
1874	7.22	13.69	20.91	1110	70	59	24	83	13
1875	7.86	14.66	22.52	1196	86	67	36	103	17
1876	8.86	14.79	23.65	1322	126	128	20	148	22
1877	9.36	15.38	24.74	1346	24	24	10	34	10
1878	9.62	16.00	25.62	1389	43	20	20	40	−3
1879	10.03	17.06	27.09	1421	32	0	0	30	−2
1880	11.58	17.98	29.56	1465	44	20	45	65	21
1881	12.59	18.99	31.58	1546	81	40	25	65	−16
1882	12.80	19.26	32.06	1580	34	8	25	33	−1
1883	13.11	19.98	33.09	1629	49	26	40	66	17
1884	13.56	19.70	33.26	1697	68	16	53	69	1
1885	13.87	19.70	33.57	1732	33	0	32	32	−3
1886	14.03	19.27	33.30	1767	35	0	45	45	10
1887	14.10	19.34	33.44	1795	28	0	35	35	7
1888	14.56	20.00	35.16	1822	27	0	26	26	−1
1889	15.41	22.22	37.63	1844	22	0	32	32	10
1890	15.40	23.66	39.06	1926	82	60	47	107	25
1891	16.12	24.78	40.90	2020	94	78	35	113	19
1892	16.48	25.00	41.48	2172	152	142	30	172	20
1893	16.04	22.00	38.04	2217	45	65	20	85	40
1894	16.22	24.41	40.63	2227	10	0	30	30	20
1895	16.34	24.32	40.66	2252	25	25	20	45	20
1896	16.84	25.10	41.94	2293	41	35	15	50	9
1897	17.70	26.18	43.88	2360	67	65	23	88	21
1898	18.36	27.71	46.07	2360	0	0	23	23	23
1899	18.98	28.39	47.37	2507	147	158	21	179	32
1900	19.39	28.63	48.02	2615	108	92	18	110	2
1901	19.90	28.16	48.06	2709	94	88	15	103	9
1902	20.42	27.04	47.46	2782	73	57	22	79	6
1903	21.74	25.16	46.90	2790	8	0	41	41	33
1904	22.69	24.75	47.44	2790	0	0	36	36	36
1905	22.56	25.35	47.92	2790	0	0	31	31	31
1906	23.29	26.32	49.61	2790	0	0	30	30	30
1907	23.39	27.52	50.91	2790	0	0	46	46	46
1908	23.26	26.33	49.59	2800	10	0	26	26	16
1909	22.52	26.09	48.61	2800	0	0	14	14	14
1910	22.59	26.31	48.90	2800	0	0	0	0	0
1911	22.44	26.31	48.83	2800	0	0	2	2	2
1912	21.09	25.19	46.28	2800	0	0	0	0	0
1913				2925*	(125)	0	0	0	(125)
1914				2925	0	0	0	0	0
1915				2924	−1	0	0	0	−1
1916				2924	0	0	0	0	0
1917				2921	−3	0	15	15	12
1918				2927	−6	0	28	28	22
1919				2926	−1	0	23	23	22
1920				2927	1	0	35	35	34
1921				2927	0	45	29	74	74
1922				2925*	−2	5	16	21	19
TOTAL						1627	1248	2865	

**Excluding 94 LT & SR locomotives*

NB Train mileage figures from 1913 would not bear valid comparison with those for 1870-1912 owing to (1) a change in mode of compilation of statistics and (2) absorption of LT & SR.

The so-called withdrawal figures are the difference between the number of new locomotives and the net increase. It sometimes has a negative value! Apart from this, the withdrawal figures are purely theoretical as many engines could pass into duplicate stock.

PRE-1907 MIDLAND RAILWAY LOCOMOTIVE NUMBERING

Before 1907 the running numbers of Midland locomotives reflected the fact that new locomotives were charged either to capital or revenue account. Those built to capital account were given the next available block of entirely new numbers, the highest thus pre-1907, being the first Johnson Class 3 0–6–0s, Nos. 2736-2740 of 1903. The remaining forty-five 0–6–0s built pre-1907 were charged to revenue account and numbered consecutively 140-184. 'Revenue' engines more often, but not invariably, were given low, two- and three-digit numbers, where possible taking consecutive blocks of numbers formerly carried by Kirtley engines. The latter might well still be in existence but transferred to duplicate stock, signified by an 'A' suffix, which were not included in six-monthly and annual returns. The number of new engines charged to revenue account year by year varied considerably, but very often corresponded closely or exactly with the apparent number of withdrawals computed by comparing successive annual returns and taking into account new construction. Locomotives charged to capital account reflected the net annual increase in reported locomotive stock, which continued to rise until 1903.

The complex matter of duplicate stock seems to have been a method by which the Midland (and other railways which indulged in similar practices) were able 'to have their cake and eat it'. As far as the accountants were concerned, an old locomotive was no longer on the books and a replacement could be authorised, although in reality, the former was still in active use. It was possibly to assist this process that some Kirtley locomotives were transferred from capital to duplicate and back to capital stock in only a matter of months! To complicate the issue still further, a few engines, some of the Johnson 0–4–0 'brewery tanks', were actually built new to duplicate stock. Surprisingly, some of this class had unusually short lives, No. 1429 lasting only from 1890 to 1905.

It is interesting to note that the great majority of the locomotives charged to revenue account were Derby-built, and included most of the 4–2–2s, all the Deeley 990 and 1000 4–4–0s, and the 0–6–4Ts Almost all the Johnson Class 2 0–6–0s were charged to capital, as were most of the 0–4–4Ts and 0–6–0Ts.

MR REVENUE ACCOUNT

Year	*No Locos Re-boilered*	*No Locos Built to Revenue A/C*	*No Withdrawals* (Apparent)*
1888	105	3	1
1889	111	8	10
1890	120	25	25
1891	125	19	19
1892	114	30	20
1893	68	20	40
1894	82	28	20
1895	76	22	20
1896	91	12	9
1897	100	21	21
1898	128	20	23
1899	154	20	32
1900	155	10	2
1901	172	10	10
1902	165	10	6
1903	139	35	33
1904	131	34	36
1905	108	31	31
1906	139	26	30
1907	144	46	46
1908	66	18	16
1909	93	12	14
1910	120	0	0
1911	120	2	2
1912	105	0	0
1913	120	0	0
1914	120	0	0

SOME FURTHER THOUGHTS ON MIDLAND LOCOMOTIVE DESIGN

In Volume 2 we speculated more than once about the reasons behind the slow move of the Midland to larger locomotives at the end of the Johnson period and suggested that this may have had something to do with the Board policy of the Midland Railway. At the same time, we also inferred, at least in part, that Johnson himself may not always have been convinced of the need for such developments, hence his perseverance with the slim-boilered 4–4–0s and bogie singles almost to the end of the 19th century. Some of our friends have taken us to task for making these, admittedly subjective comments but it would seem that we were not entirely wrong in our thoughts. It now seems likely that Johnson was mostly prompted to make the changes to larger engines by his chief draughtsman but that even after these new designs had begun to appear, the dead hand of the Midland Board was not entirely absent.

The precise truth probably lies somewhere in the middle, but there were many interesting 'goings on' at Derby during the first decade or two of the 20th century and some of them reflect more credit on the Derby drawing office than latter-day commentators have sometimes been prepared to admit. What is certain is that had even some of the drawing office ideas reached fruition, the Midland would have had a rather better locomotive fleet to hand over to the LMS, in terms of design quality, than in fact was the case. Furthermore, though much of the really interesting activity stems from the Deeley and early Fowler period, it actually started at the end of the Johnson era. The brief survey which follows gives an interesting insight into what might have been; what is perhaps most surprising is the extent to which Derby could have pre-empted by almost twenty years some of the developments which eventually the LMS was to introduce.

S. W. Johnson had produced the largest and penultimate British 'single' 4–2–2 design in 1899, the celebrated *Princess of Wales*. The ultimate was the H. Pollitt Great

Central Class 13 4—2—2 of 1900, which dimensionally bore a close resemblance, not least the large firegrate of 24.5 sq. ft. Both designs, like the MR and GCR 4—4—0s which directly preceded them, had W. M. Smith patent piston valves beneath the cylinders. Now serving as chief locomotive draughtsman to the North Eastern Railway at Gateshead, Smith had been an assistant to Johnson on the Great Eastern Railway over forty years earlier, and in January 1901 his son John, already at Derby, was promoted to the corresponding post there. Smith's presence brought a new vitality to Johnson's closing years, which was first manifested in the Belpaire '700' class 4—4—0s, closely followed by the very large three-cylinder 4—4—0s Nos. 2631-5 compounded on W. M. Smith's system. (A sharp rise in the price of coal in mid-1900 might finally have persuaded Johnson.) On the freight side, just before Johnson's retirement at the end of 1903, ten 0—8—0s were authorised. These would have had outside cylinders and would have closely resembled the NER Class T 0—8—0s, but regrettably they were subsequently cancelled by the Board. Whether this decision was because they were thought too big or too expensive is not known. From then on until 1920, 0—8—0 and 2—8—0 schemes were regularly drawn up, of which the only actual manifestation was the six Somerset & Dorset 2—8—0s in 1914. From this, it is clear that the Midland's obsession with six-coupled goods engines was not the fault of its locomotive draughtsmen and designers.

Johnson was succeeded in office by R. M. Deeley who was a man of many parts including geologist, genealogist, meteorologist, and tribologist. Deeley almost immediately proposed superheating, two years before its first actual appearance on the GWR and LYR, but this, too, was rejected by the Midland Board, this time on account of the £50 per engine royalty fee which would be demanded! A whole range of heavy suburban passenger tank engine proposals were also drawn up, including advanced (for the time) outside-cylinder 2—6—4 and 4—6—4 arrangements. It was therefore somewhat ironic that the design selected, the distinctive 'Flatiron' 0—6—4T, which amounted to a slightly larger wheeled tank engine version of the Johnson Class 3 0—6—0, should have proved so disappointing. It was even more ironic that the eventual and successful design of big passenger tank (the LMS built Fowler 2—6—4T and its successors) turned out to be, in large part, a 'replay' of ideas which had not found favour at Derby almost twenty years earlier! The leading light in these matters was almost certainly James Clayton and he must have had a frustrating time!

In like manner, little consideration was given to producing a more powerful express passenger engine, other than Deeley's proposed four-cylinder compound 4—6—0 in 1907. In that same year he produced a simple expansion equivalent to the compounds, No. 999. Nine more were subsequently built, and all were later superheated. With short direct steam ports and unusually large grates of 28.4 sq. ft., larger in fact than most contemporary 4—6—0s, these might have shaped up as potential equivalents of the celebrated LNWR 'George V' 4—4—0s, but there is no record of any truly outstanding performances. Some measure of what might otherwise have been possible with these engines was later provided on the South Eastern & Chatham Railway, to which James Clayton transferred from Derby in 1913 to become chief draughtsman. He thereupon masterminded the outstanding D1 and E1 rebuilds, which incorporated long travel piston valves and superheaters to great effect. On the SE & CR, as on the Midland, locomotive development was severely circumscribed by stringent weight restrictions, but at least this company had the good sense to let James Clayton have his head and his influence (via Maunsell) went on into Southern Railway days as well.

Thus it was that on the Midland Railway by the end of 1922, only about 12½ per cent of its locomotive stock was superheated (which included only about half the 45 compound 4—4—0s) compared with 25 per cent on the LNWR. The seemingly outward conservatism of the Midland in locomotive matters was thus not a consequence of an unprogressive drawing office; given its head, it was almost the equal of any of its contemporaries, as was testified to by the actual production of the S & D 2—8—0s in 1914, and the eventual appearance of the four-cylinder Lickey 0—10—0 in 1919, delayed by World War I. Stringent economies and weight restrictions imposed by the Civil Engineer, plus perhaps a less than perfect understanding of steam locomotive development by the MR Board, had, between them, frustrated attempts to progress beyond the seemingly endless procession of 4—4—0s and 0—6—0s on the Midland main line.

Thus, although the London & North Western Railway (which reached roughly the same geographical extremities as did the Midland) built no fewer than 680 4—6—0s and 572 0—8—0s, the Midland did not operate a single example of either. However, it is interesting to note that latterly the Midland boasted more tender locomotives than either the LNWR or GWR. Its totals were, of course, dominated by the 0—6—0, of which the final count was precisely 1,600, or almost one quarter of the national total, in 1922. Such other tender types as the MR then operated in total also dwarfed those of other companies, i.e. 4—4—0 (386), 2—4—0 (245), 4—2—2 (43). Interestingly, the same applied to the 0—4—4T (226) and even the 0—6—4Ts (40), but the 0—6—0T total came a poor second, at 353, to the c.1,100 such engines on the GWR. In addition the Lickey 0—10—0 was the only ten-coupled engine operating in Britain for 25 years.

APPENDIX
LOCOMOTIVE BUILDING COSTS
by C. P. Atkins

Monetary inflation was practically unknown pre-1914, but commodity prices could and did fluctuate widely in the short term. This was reflected in locomotive building costs, of which an excellent barometer is the cost of MR inside-frame 0–6–0s. Of very simple design, these were built in hundreds over a period of almost fifty years and incorporated during that time only two major design changes (in 1903 and 1911) which had no apparent impact on cost.

The typical cost of a Johnson Class 2 0–6–0 was around £2,250, which in practice fell to just below the £2,000 mark in 1886 during a period of industrial stagnation, but rose sharply between 1897 and 1901, a period of intense industrial activity, peaking at just over £3,000 per engine. This would have reflected the contemporary heavy demand for, and hence higher cost of materials, especially iron, steel and copper. The price in 1902 fell sharply back to £2,500 apiece. If this is reduced to cost per ton deadweight, it is interesting to note that the cost of Midland engines usually came just above that of LNWR locomotives built at Crewe and just below that of LYR engines built at Horwich. Prices for all three railways followed the same pattern, normally fluctuating between £40 and £50 per ton between 1875 and 1914, except for a brief peak of £60 per ton during 1900-1901.

Inflation took off with a vengeance during the latter half of World War I, and the price of new Class 4 0–6–0s built at Derby rose sharply. The two prototypes built in 1911 were costed at £2,432 each (£42 per ton) whereas those built in 1921 cost just three times as much at £7,484 each (£1.30 per ton). By 1922 the price was falling again, trends which were mirrored in the cost of LNWR 0–8–0s built at Crewe and GWR 2–6–0s at Swindon over precisely the same period.

The prices are taken from LMS Engine History Cards which show that at any given time the cost of a Johnson 0–4–4T was almost the same as that for an 0–6–0. 0–6–0Ts cost between £1,650 and £2,250.

The unit cost of slender-boilered 4–4–0s varied between £2,700 and £3,300. No figures are available for the first ten 'Belpaires', of 1900-1901, which were therefore probably the most expensive MR 4–4–0s of all, but the later examples are consistently quoted at £2,794 each. The original Johnson Compounds are all given at £3,340 each, despite the alterations made to the latter three, and the subsequent Deeley variants built 1905-8 are all stated to have been £3,388. With their smaller tenders, one would have expected the Deeley engines to have been rather cheaper, and one has to admit to the consistency of some of the official costs making them somewhat suspect, but they are a good indication.

A Johnson 0–4–0ST in 1897 cost a princely £895. Its Deeley successor in 1907 cost £1,361, of which the 1921 builds cost £3,889 each. The one-off 0–10–0 cost £8,458 in 1919, not so very much more than a production 0–6–0 only two years later. No figures survive for the 4–2–2s, Deeley '990' 4–4–0s or 0–6–4Ts, on account of their comparatively 'early' demise by Midland standards, for all had gone by 1939. It is interesting to note that the original Johnson 0–6–0 of 1875 remained in service until 1957, and that it and its 1,126 successors (Nos. 2901-4026) represented a total investment of around £3½ million. It is intriguing to speculate how much revenue they generated for the Midland Railway and its successors prior to final extinction in 1965.

THE BUILDING COST OF MR 0–6–0 LOCOMOTIVES 1875-1922*

	1907 Nos.	*Date*	*Cost per Engine*
Class 2	2900-3019	1875-6	£2,578
	3020-3113	1878-1883	£2,293
	3114-3149	1884-5	£2,129
	3150-3159	1886	£1,965
	3160-3189	1887	£2,218
	3190-3199	1888	£2,649
	3200-3259	1890	£2,460
	3260-3299	1891	£2,192
	3300-3307	1891	£2,460
	3308-3339	1892	£2,649
	3340-3369	1891	£2,460
	3370-3399	1892	£2,361
	3400-3409	1893	£2,649
	3410-3429	1892	£2,361
	3430-3459	1893	£2,192
	3460-3469	1894	£2,460
	3470-3569	1896-7	£2,221
	3570-3590	1899	£2,563
	3591-3599	1900	£3,028
	3600-3629	1899	£2,838
	3630-3649	1900	£3,028
	3650-3669	1900	£2,693
	3670-3689	1901	£3,028
	3690-3709	1901	£2,693
	3710-3737	1901	£3,028
	3738-3764	1902	£2,460
Class 3	3765-3804	1903-4	£2,460
	3805-3834	1906-8	£2,649
Class 4	3835-3836	1911	£2,432
	3837-3851	1917	£3,928
	3852-1379	1918	£4,864
	3880-3901	1919	£6,174
	3902-3935	1920	£6,548
	3936-3966	1921	£7,484
	3967-3986	1922	£6,735
	3987-4013	1921	£7,484
	4014-4026	1922	£6,735
	None built during 1923		
(LMS	4027-4034	1924	£4,600)
(	4035-4056	1925	£4,114)

*These figures are taken from surviving LMS Engine History Cards.

AN INDEX TO ILLUSTRATIONS OF MIDLAND RAILWAY TANK ENGINES IN VOLUMES 1 & 3

'Old' refers to a pre-1907 number.